LETTERS TO RISING LEADERS

On God, Soul, Love and Leadership in a Wounded World

TOM MOHR

Receiving the burning torch of leadership may well bring pain. But, when received in service of Greater Love, it is small price for Greater Gain.

Acclaim for The Rising Leader Series Letters

As a Jesuit who has committed many years of ministry to the accompaniment and spiritual formation of college students, I find Tom Mohr's *Rising Leader Series* letters both challenging and nourishing. He infuses life experiences and current global crises and realities with his Christian faith, offering substantive reflections. Tom focuses on those willing to become leaders living the Gospel call and dedicated to fostering healing and wholeness in our world. As he writes, "To be most fully Christian is to study, to pray, to search out our sins, to seek forgiveness, to welcome God's grace, to deepen our sense of connectedness to God and all things, to form a conscience, to hear our call and then to go into the world and serve— animated by a gentleness of spirit." I imagine that all who absorb his message will find themselves desiring to respond to that call from God to be agents of change, living with courage and compassion as they commit to making God's dream for humanity ever more apparent. I'm grateful to Tom for this gift.

Jack Treacy, S.J.
University Relations Chaplain
Santa Clara University

In his *Rising Leader Series* letters, Tom Mohr deftly integrates core values that are too often misunderstood to be oppositional: faith and deeds, hope and realism, leadership and humility, individual responsibility and the common good, unity and diversity, time-honored truth and innovative progress, the upward slope of influence and the downward slope of genuine servanthood. While the reader might expect to find only tension and discord between these values, Tom's reflections bring alignment and harmony. These letters are cups of refreshing water for our parched hearts and our purpose-thirsty society.

Rev. Rob Fredrickson, Associate Minister
Ozaukee Congregational Church
Grafton, Wisconsin

At a time when we face a crisis of leadership in our society, and solving big problems can seem impossible, Tom Mohr challenges the next generation of leaders to think more broadly about their roles as leaders and move beyond focusing on achieving the narrowest of outcomes. He writes, "[b]ecome the capable, ethical leader our world needs. Planet health, geopolitical stability, failed-state recovery, democracy's health, community well-being, interpersonal connectedness and personal soulfulness -- all are put in peril without you." Whether faith guides you or not, there are lessons in Tom's letters that will help any future leader find greater purpose in their leadership and identify ways to build strategies that will broaden their impact.

Willie Hernandez
General Counsel, International
The Coca-Cola Company
Atlanta, GA

The thoughts in this book will challenge you! Get ready to listen and reflect and act. Our world will become a better place and you will be a better person when you internalize Tom Mohr's insightful thoughts. Read daily as a devotional, or weekly, and just savor and be inspired by the messages. These words are a gift.

Maureen Laird-Hayes
Plymouth, MN

I have been honored to have the opportunity to work with Tom Mohr and have him as my mentor, and each week I have enjoyed reading his *Rising Leader Series* letters. As a rising leader myself, the content of the letters resonates enormously with me – they have helped me self-reflect and take a deeper dive into the core values that drive my leadership style, as I always strive to be a better, more compassionate leader every day.

In Tom's *Rising Leader Series*, he provides a clear outline of the seven disciplines of goodness (piety, decency, civility, charity, democracy, diplomacy and sustainability) that are needed to make a good and selfless leader and emphasizes the importance of having a strong relationship with God along that journey. Through my work with Tom and his letters, I have grown to become a more empathetic leader and now have a greater love for humanity and the world.

Kevin Miller
CEO, Gr0
Los Angeles

Over the past year, I have been inspired by Tom Mohr's weekly *Rising Leader Series* letters. These weekly readings and reflections were just what I needed, since it is my passion to create and implement visions that enable change, especially regarding outreach to others in need. Through roles in the private sector, academia and in several churches, I have often been the one leading the change. This last year, it was time to "recharge". Timing is everything, and Tom's weekly messages helped me to pause, reflect, and to discern how my Christian faith can help me become a better leader and discover new solutions to the many challenges in our troubled world.

The letters are well organized, promoting reflection in four dimensions: "Who is God?"; "Who am I?"; "Where is the Need?"; and "What is my Call?". As a lifelong, serial entrepreneur I advocate becoming part of the solution, not the problem. This book will be a true call to action for all of us who seek to serve.

Arthur A. Boni, Ph.D.
John R. Thorne Distinguished Career Professor of Entrepreneurship, Emeritus
Tepper School of Business, Carnegie Mellon University
Napa, California

Rarely does one encounter inspirational ideas that so fluidly, holistically—and with hope—integrate the spiritual and the practical. Yet Tom Mohr's *Rising Leader Series* letters, and the songs that accompany them, do just that.

Having held leadership positions in higher education for two decades, first on the executive team of a national organization, and twice as a university president at faith-based institutions, I found that being a good and caring leader had become increasingly difficult over time, when it should have become easier. I firmly believe that is because we have lost our way as a society, and that we have lost touch with the values that undergird excellent leadership, making authentic leadership and leadership of conscience an increasingly uphill struggle.

This is a central premise to Tom's offering to future leaders. He recognizes that the "world is in deep hunger," and that we need leaders who benefit from spiritual support and grace. In his letters, Tom brings God and self-reflection to the heart of leadership, and thankfully offers his own reflections as tools for mentoring new leaders. Even as a retired leader I find Tom's letters generative and inspirational.

MaryAnn Baenninger, Ph.D.
Retired President, College of Saint Benedict, Saint Joseph, MN, and Drew University, Madison,
NJ

My first introduction to Tom's heart and intellect was via our association together with the Kairos Prison Ministry, in a Level 4 prison in California. Here Tom worked alongside me, helping to lead prisoners to God. He was on the music team. I later learned about Tom's work in business leadership, which prompted me to acquire most of his books. I have given them to friends and family for their own leadership development. Tom brings a unique combination of insight, personal experiences, leadership experiences, writing skills and mentoring skills that prepares him well to challenge and encourage existing and future leaders.

In Tom's *Rising Leader Series* letters, he combines these gifts with his love of God to offer a refreshing and thought provoking perspective on faith and leadership. Now that these weekly writings have been consolidated into this book, readers will be able to explore his core concepts: our need for God, our responsibility to others (especially generations to come), and the call to Servant Leadership. In his letters, Tom offers unique insights into the workings of God in our lives. He reminds us that God guides us always.... if we let Him. This is especially important for our next generation of leaders, who must take up the challenge to improve our world.

Dave Roberts
SVSP Kairos Board Member
Los Gatos, CA

My friend, Tom Mohr, came into my life 30 years ago as a young rising leader himself. Back then, we were on the board of a nonprofit organization that had a leadership crisis which threatened its very existence. I saw Tom stand up and inspire others to take bold and urgent steps to keep the doors open. Thanks to Tom standing in the gap, that organization today is a recognized leader in teaching life, leadership, and employment skills to teens of color in Minneapolis/ St. Paul.

Tom is passionate about the need for leaders to first bring their hearts to God and then their gifts to the world around them. Tom lives his life with the faith and courage to do the right thing. He has prepared himself for his servant leadership role through a life of prayer, study, and action. This book provides his thought provoking guidance to rising leaders on the preparation needed to be leaders of goodness.

Tom Meyer
Owner, Home Energy Center
Plymouth, MN

As humans grapple with crises of climate, divisiveness and faith, many of us are asking how we can make a difference. Tom Mohr's Letters to Rising Leaders reminds us of the criticality of leadership. Writing to the next generation of leaders, Tom provides a roadmap and framework for leaders to strengthen the faith that necessarily undergirds effective, ethical leadership. To become an ethical leader requires a journey of the soul -- to find God and commit to ethical impact. Through God we can find and anchor ourselves to prepare ourselves to contribute to all that God loves. God is everywhere and in everyone: those we agree with and those we don't; those like us and those not like us. Tom challenges us to become a leader, healer of division and contributor in a world filled with need. And Tom's direct style, delivered with powerful, authentic and vulnerable stories, make for easy, uplifting reading.

David Kopp
Former CEO, Healthline Media
Los Altos, CA

My first encounter with Tom Mohr's *Rising Leader Series* letters came through my office emails at the church where I am a pastoral assistant. The first "Rising Leader" letter that I read (which was not the first in the series) inspired me to find and read all the previous ones, as well as look forward to reading the ones that appeared among my emails each week. The *Rising Leader Series* letters provide inspirational CPR for one's soul. They call individual spirits to bring the love of God back to life in this world. They deliver a summons to shrug off apathy and desperation and share the gifts and fruits of the Holy Spirit one has with those who are unfamiliar with them. The "Rising Leader" letters offer sustenance to those called to evangelize the Good News of life in Christ in today's world.

Mary Anne White
Pastoral Assistant, Holy Rosary & St. John Catholic Church
Reynoldsburg, Ohio

I get all kinds of emails trying to "sell" me the "latest and the best in cutting edge ministry resources". While many I have learned to delete with a quick push of the keyboard button, this Rising Leaders Series caught my attention. I remember reading it, re-reading it for fuller reflection, and then creating a "Tom Mohr" folder where I could save it.

Tom's shared journey and experience resonate with the larger questions of life and faith that are urgent and important in the cultural context we find ourselves in. When public "leaders" say or do something that I would discipline my child for, I recognize that we urgently need to reclaim what it means to be a real leader. Tom addresses this in his writings. My encouragement is for people to allow this book to become more than a one-time read. May it become a dialogue for all who desire and seek to mature in their own lives and, prayerfully, become a leaven in the world that is so desperately in need.

Rev. Dr. Scott L. Crane
Presbytery of Lake Michigan
(Honorably Retired)

Tom Mohr's *Rising Leader Series* is a powerful and compelling call to action. Now more than ever, we need moral and enlightened action to save ourselves and our planet. Tom's thoughtful and inclusive step-by-step approach serves as a path to cultivating and nurturing the inner leader in each of us. Read these letters, be guided by their message, and help change the world.

Dr. Vol Van Dalsem
Los Altos, CA

As a CEO, I am constantly seeking out new ways to improve my leadership skills and make a positive impact in my organization. Tom Mohr's *Rising Leader Series* has been an invaluable resource in this journey, providing valuable insights and practical guidance on the importance of ethical leadership in times of crisis. Not only has this series helped me to be a more effective leader within my company, but it has also been relevant to my work as a physician, where the choices and actions of leaders can have a significant impact on the well-being of patients. I highly recommend this book to anyone looking to inspire and motivate themselves and others towards positive change.

Dr. Zwade Marshall, MD
Co-Founder and CEO,

Doc2Doc Lending;
Founder & Chief Medical Officer,
Regenerative Spine & Pain Specialists

I am deeply touched by Tom Mohr's *Rising Leader Series*. In stories, poems and songs, he calls for a new generation of capable and ethical leaders to rise up to the challenges of our world. Leadership is not a position nor status or title, it is a service that serves the better good of our society and people. As our world is in crisis, we need a new generation of ethical leaders to take the lead. To quote John Wooden, "The leader's attitude, conscious, and subconscious, inevitably becomes the attitude of those they lead." Tom Mohr's *Rising Leader Series* shows the path to ethical leadership. It is a refreshing read.

Helen Yu
Founder & CEO
Tigon Advisory Corp.

LETTERS TO RISING LEADERS

On God, Soul, Love and Leadership in a Wounded World

TOM MOHR

This book is dedicated to
Lionel Charles Mohr

Leader of goodness
Wonderful father
Now in Heaven

Thank you, Dad

How To Read This Book

As Fredrick Buechner once said, "The place God calls you to is the place where your deep gladness and the world's deep hunger meet." The world needs you, good leader. Capable, ethical you. In this book, it is my goal to help you do the interior work necessary to become a leader of goodness. Leaders of goodness can arise from any faith tradition or set of beliefs. But here you will find the Christian path to goodness. Jesus asks you to let Him in, so that together you and He can do the soul work that prepares you to be His hands and feet in the world.

This book, Letters to Rising Leaders, is composed of an Introduction, plus the 52 letters that comprised the *Rising Leader Series*– one for each week of the year. The letters are organized into four quarters of thirteen letters each. The first quarter of the year takes up the question, *"Who is God?"*. The second asks, *"Who am I?"*. The third, *"Where's the Need?"*. And the fourth, *"What's my Call?"*.

Sprinkled throughout the book, you'll also find the lyrics for the twelve songs that were part of the original *Rising Leader Series* (along with instructions about how to find and hear them online). I hope these songs also contribute to the formation of your heart.

There are many ways to read this book. You could read it once a week, roughly following the quarterly timeline– which means that (unless you happen to pick it up in the first week of January) you will start somewhere in the middle. Or you could read it from the beginning, once a week, without concern for keeping in alignment with the quarterly calendar. Or you could read it front-to-back at your leisure, over the course of a week or a month. All of these methods are perfectly fine.

Regardless of how you choose to read it, though, read the Introduction first. This will set the foundation. Along the way, take time to pray. I encourage you to take a moment with God in prayer every time you finish reading a letter. God is over the moon about you. He believes in you. He seeks a close, intimate relationship with you.

It is my fervent hope that as you read this book, you will be inspired to welcome God into your soul. That over time you will begin to sense– from depth to depth– His love, truth, grace and call. So that you might begin to shine ever more brightly from the inside out. And that then you might step forward to serve– one more beacon of goodness in a world starved for light.

Introduction

Great leaders can move mountains. This is the first important thing, because mountains must be moved. Never in history has it been more true: leadership matters. It is why, to you and next-generation leaders like you, I say this:

You are the most important person in the world right now.

The second important thing is that our world is in crisis. Planet sustainability... geopolitical stability... the health of our democracy... our respect for diversity... the connectedness of our communities... the strength of our houses of worship... big rips have emerged in the fabric of our most precious human systems. As any student of leadership knows: once complex systems become dysfunctional, they cannot be rebalanced without big, sustained, coordinated interventions. That takes leadership-- now on an unprecedented global scale, with time as our enemy.

We are on the cusp of a forty-year period in which the choices and actions of humanity's leaders will determine our path, for good or ill. Will the next generation of rising leaders respond to God's call to meet the world's woundedness with love? Will they (you) make the sacrifices necessary to climb the path towards healing? Or will they (you) continue to act as so many of our current and past leaders have done-- from self-centered motivations? You, rising leader, will choose.

Which leads us to the third important thing. To do good, our leaders must be good. If we are to turn the tide, ethical leadership is critical. And that doesn't just happen. It takes a relationship with God, formed through the discipline of piety.

Why Now

We humans haven't changed much over the past three hundred years. At least in terms of virtue and vice. Ever since humanity's emergence out of the mists of time, we have been endowed by our

Creator with two gifts: original goodness and free will. In our goodness, we have exhibited a great capacity to love, to empathize, to sacrifice, to rescue, to heal. But also, in our manic struggle to survive and procreate, we have often seized that freedom of our will to stray from our original goodness. Gripped by fear or compulsion, we've shrunk our circles of care-- turning inward to self, tribe, nation-- at others' expense. In fear, we've distrusted. We've demonized the "other". We've hoarded. We've acted with indifference towards the least among us. We've lusted for power. We've exploited without thought of the impact. Yes, we humans are (and always have been) both saints and sinners.

But, to flip an old saying on its head, the more things stay the same the more they change. A certain change-- one that has emerged over the past three hundred years-- is of the greatest consequence to the future of our species. This change is the emergence and ever-rising power of science to transform.

Born out of the Enlightenment, the scientific method gifted our world with three centuries of ever-accelerating invention. We have doubled life expectancy. We have wired the globe. We have become acquainted with all the world's cultures-- their values, norms, arts and rituals. We have built global supply chains. We have rationalized crop-growing, so as to feed the world. Humanity's knowledge resides in our iPhones. We are digitally connected to people and experiences like never before. When a global pandemic hit, we created powerful, life-saving vaccines and distributed them around the world with unprecedented speed. Who can deny the power of science to do good? It is all around us. Yes, science has been a force for great good in the world.

But science has also brought us the atom bomb and bioweapons. In just two days we wiped out two cities: Hiroshima and Nagasaki. In just two hundred years we have brought our entire planet from pristine health to the brink of ecological disaster. We've built the machines that have accelerated destruction of forests, leveled mountains for coal, cast ever more carbon into the atmosphere, and raked our oceans free of fish. Digital connectedness has helped us amplify our hate. Sophisticated artificial intelligence algorithms now tempt us towards our worst impulses. Caught in a continuous digital stream of distractions, we've lost simple human connectivity; never-ending images of suffering, scandalizing, lusting and grandstanding have left us empty and emotionally anesthetized. And meanwhile, as humanity wallows in ethical apathy and confusion, artificial intelligence speeds the pace of learning itself, spinning science forward faster and faster.

This too is science.

Our volatile human cocktail of virtue and vice, saintliness and sinfulness hasn't changed over the past three hundred years-- but through scientific advances, the tools available to us to act upon our virtue and vice have. And so, like never before in human history, our need for virtuous, ethical, selfless servant leaders to take the reins– to build up the guardrails– is now absolute. It's no overstatement to say that without you and leaders like you rising to this challenge, all across the globe, humanity will continue its slide towards the abyss.

Can you see, good leader, why this all comes back to you, and why the moment is now? We need leaders who know what goodness is, who are good themselves, and who will place science in service of goodness. Without ethically grounded leadership, science becomes weaponized by vice. Leaders of goodness are called by God to rise– to run to the need and to stand in the gap.

Why You

It strikes me that the challenge your generation faces is even greater than that faced by the Greatest Generation. Yes, my parents' generation dug out of the Great Depression, confronted epic evil and rose to the call to sacrifice everything (75 million lives; the wealth of nations; years of dashed hopes; years of blood, sweat and tears) so that the bell of freedom could still ring. The mind can barely comprehend what they did for us.

But now, all we hold dear is on the line. The work that must be done to heal our planet, nation, communities, churches and hearts is epic.

If humanity is to turn the tide, it will take decades of selfless, dedicated leadership, all across the globe, from senior leaders at the top of change-driving organizational pyramids, to operational and functional leaders, and all the way down to those who lead from the front line.

There's only one answer: you.

My generation certainly isn't the answer. It is we who handed you the world in this condition. It is we who are responsible for much of the shallowness and selfishness of our age. On behalf of my generation, I offer amends. I'm sorry.

No, humanity's hope rests on your shoulders. You are the one called to a sacrifice different in kind from that of the Greatest Generation, but perhaps even more significant. For you, it must be in a radical reprioritization of what matters, a discovery of connectedness to and care for generations present and future, and a passionate lifelong dedication to the rescue work that must be done. Yes, you are our future. You have what it takes to rise to the moment. But this kind of sacrificial leadership won't just happen. It requires a journey of the soul.

Why God

We can't do it alone. On our own, we are too selfish-- too prideful-- too preoccupied. On our own, we cannot untangle the soul knots that hold back our return to our true selves. It takes a journey of the heart, with God as our companion and guide.

God teaches us to value ourselves, and all else that He loves-- both those we agree with and those we don't; fellow country-mates and those in other countries; those richer and poorer; those of races different from our own; those in crisis both near and far. With new eyes, our care for future generations grows as well. A soul journey with God leads inexorably through and beyond ourselves. It draws us into His hurting world to serve.

Why Care

Everything is connected, everything is alive, everything emanates love. From the atomic particle, to the leaping deer in the forest, to all humanity, to our planets and stars and everything in between, we are connected, with love. Once we see this truth, we realize that dishonor to anyone or anything is dishonor to ourselves. We begin to expand our circle of care. We become committed to goodness.

Why This Book

The world needs leaders of goodness– leaders grounded in God and ready to serve. This takes discipline and commitment. I've written the fifty-two letters that make up this book to encourage and challenge rising leaders like you. It is my prayer that you will embark on a soul journey with God, and then will take up God's call to love and heal the world.

It requires a new worldview. I believe that to see our connectedness, and to bind science to goodness and forsake its use for evil, the world's rising leaders must step into— even dedicate their lives to— seven disciplines of goodness:

- *Piety*, so that in our relationship with God, we may return our souls to balance

- *Decency*, so that in each of our encounters, by bestowing upon our neighbors the dignity we expect others to bestow upon ourselves, we keep human connectedness in balance

- *Civility*, so that in our diverse communities, debate will lead towards balance

- *Charity*, so that from neighbor to failed nation state we might help the hurting regain their balance

- *Democracy*, so as to retain national social and political balance

- *Diplomacy*, so as to help nation states stay in geopolitical balance

- *Sustainability*, so as to bring the planet back into balance

Think of these disciplines as a ladder. To climb, you need to gain solid footing on the first step– piety:

In this series of letters, good leader, I will offer you the Christian path to ethical leadership. But we must appreciate that the Christian path is not the only path to goodness. We live in a pluralistic world. Good people, good leaders are all around us. In our healing work, we are called to journey together with all people of goodwill. This "we're-all-in-it-together" way of thinking is Christian (in the "what would Jesus do" sense).

The weekly *Rising Leader Series* letters are organized by quarter:

- **First Quarter**: Who is God? What does He have to do with leadership?

- **Second Quarter**: Who am I? What soul work must I do to become a selfless servant leader?

- **Third Quarter**: Where's the need? Planet, democracy, community, race relations, houses of worship-- what's the work to be done?

- **Fourth Quarter**: What's my call? Where do I begin?

My letters to you constitute a supportive challenge. I offer it to you and all like you who will become our next generation of leaders:

Leader of goodness,

Go in faith

To love and heal the world

Ready to begin? Return to God. It's a good first step on your quest to save the world.

Table of Contents

FIRST QUARTER:
Who is God?

LETTERS TO RISING LEADERS

Week 1 -- Abba Father

O SAP OF LOVE

In You I live and move and have my being
Connected as the branch is to the vine
O Sap of Love so warm, so strong, so freeing
That joins eternal Yours with finite mine

Though in my soul through wheat still springs the weed
Though in my heart the shadows still remain
Your grace has lifted me beyond my deeds
And planted me upon a higher plain

Today I offer far-from-perfect all
To be grafted to the world as is Your will
And so advance the purpose of my call
That I might, like Your others, bear fruit still

Thank you, blessed vine, for sap of Your grace
Emboldening my reach towards Your embrace

Rising Leader,

The world cries out for leaders who know this: God is in all, and God is love. And if God is in all, He is in us and those around us– the intimate love-bond that binds all humanity. And if God is love, He loves us just the way we are. Of course, He hopes we will become the people we were born to be. He wraps us in freedom, then prays we will make the free-will choice to return to Him and our original goodness. He prays that once we see the goodness in ourselves, we will see it in others. That we will care, and because we care we will act as healers within His Creation. This is God.

In January, my letters to you (including this one) probe the question, "Who is God the Father?". For you who will become the next generation's leaders, it is an important question– both for you and the world. Our connectedness to God is deeply correlated with our connectedness to the world. The world needs leaders who care— leaders of goodness.

I can't define God the Father in any comprehensive way, of course. But perhaps I can offer a few slivers of light. This week and for the next three, let's ponder four of these slivers: God as Abba Father, God as Creator, God as connected in space, and God as connected in time. Just four twists of an infinite divine kaleidoscope.

Today we start with Abba Father.

Our own fathers wield outsized influence on our views of God the patriarch. My father was my hero. Taskmaster, teacher, hugger, encourager, playmate, provider, protector, moral compass and occasional disciplinarian– he did his best, and I'm forever grateful.

I remember one summer day after church. I was about seven years old at the time. Dad stood by our car, chatting with a neighbor. He was wearing his Sunday best: tall, confident, and well-put-together. He had a way of putting one foot forward as he talked, turning it outward. He liked to bury one hand in his pocket while the other waved in rhythm with his talking. I remember standing there in my rumpled jacket with shirt hanging out, putting one hand in my pocket just like him, sticking one foot forward just like him, and turning the toe of my scuffed-up penny loafers out just like him. Just like him– that was my goal. My father was my sun and moon and stars. And I knew with utter certainty that he was over the moon about me.

So it is with God. God is over the moon in love with you and me. Yes, He is our moral compass and occasional disciplinarian– but He is also our encourager, teacher, provider and protector. Abba Father cares about every hair on our heads. He knows our worst, but seeks our best. He judges gently. His hand is always outstretched; His sandals are tied and He is ready to journey with us through all that life brings. God is faithful: He believes in us, even when we don't believe in Him.

But how about us? Are we faithful? Do we put one hand in our pocket just like him, and turn our foot just so? Do we seek to be just like Him? I hope so. We will never get it quite right– our shirts will hang out, our ties will remain askew, our jackets will still be rumpled and our penny loafers scuffed. But God our Father treasures our attempts.

Like a diamond, God's love has many facets. Each offers a fresh and glimmering perspective to reorder our reality. God shines His colorful light upon us in moments both ordinary and extraordinary, illuminating the most important things. He reveals Himself over the course of our lives in stages– showing us each day the light we most need. Whenever I have allowed God's light to penetrate, my perspective has changed for the better.

This is how I see Abba, our Father. He is patient, encouraging, compassionate, creative, active, forgiving and infinitely loving. He's not some cold and distant figure sitting on a mountaintop throne. He is intimately with us and in us. He loves us. He seeks a relationship with us. Will we turn to Him?

Good leader, take pause for a moment. Right now. Close your eyes; call out to Abba Father in the silence of your heart. Unlock the door of your soul and welcome Him in. Yes, as you open the door, He is sure to enter on a breeze of change— but the change He will offer will be change for the better. He will reveal Himself to you in stages, turning the kaleidoscope each time you are ready to discover a new facet of Him. All are gifts; all will bring renewal. I hope you will accept the gifts He brings you. But fair warning— He will want a hug.

Next week, we will talk about the motherly side of God.

See what great love the Father has lavished on us, that we should be called children of God! And that is what we are!-- 1 John 3:1

May Abba be with you,

Tom

Song of the Month

EVERY SHINING STAR

You see me Lord You search me Lord
You know me just the way I really am
I've wandered far I've stumbled hard
Yet still I'm part of your almighty plan

Every shining star in the heavens
Has been lit like a candle by your hand
And you God of everything know and love me
It's a miracle too vast to understand

In the secret place You knit me Lord
You created me to be your special one
And now you call You want my all
Where from your light and love can I even run?

Before a word is on my tongue Before a thought has just begun
You know. You know.
I can fly across the sea But no matter where I flee
You are. You are.

You say I'm made in your own image
But how could that possibly be true
That the soul fire of a sinful seeker
Could be lit by the great almighty you?

We've been formed in love By you above
And now you call us forth to go and give
To bring our hearts To make a start
So others might discover love and live

Before a word is on our tongues
Before a thought has just begun We'll praise Your name

In everything and everyone

FIRST QUARTER: WHO IS GOD?

We will see your kingdom come Each face Your grace

You see me Lord You search me Lord
You know me just the way I really am
And now you call You want my all
Yes, I am part of your almighty plan

Here I am I will serve Here I am My God

Search "Tom Mohr— Every Shining Star"
To find this song on YouTube, Spotify and all music platforms

LETTERS TO RISING LEADERS

Week 2 -- Creator God

HEED. LEAD. LOVE.

Caught up as howl fights howl tribe by tribe,
one million species quiet go extinct.
Too much just "me" too little "we" describe
a planet and democracy so kinked.

How smart we've been these past one hundred years--
Amazon Prime, no God, the bomb and such.
Yet all we've won has come at cost so dear:
in balance, faith, and soulful human touch.

Now systems giv'n by God are overreached.
Humanity cries out for leaders new.
To rally wealth and people to the breach,
to do what only gifted leaders do.

Servant leader, can you hear Creator's cry?
"To Me, beloved, first. Then fly. Fly. FLY!"

Rising Leader,

It is winter in Minnesota. Trees and fields are cloaked in white. In our backyard, the fox is in her foxhole. Treetops shelter squirrels as they snuggle in their nests. Flocks of people and birds have headed south for the winter– though many of both still remain. Even now in the centerpoint of winter, life thunders on. Just this morning, a family of deer ambled along the treeline out by the shed. A gaggle of wild turkeys sprinted across the road. Two down-jacket-clad women walked past me along a forest trail, talking up a storm, mist-clouds lingering in the air.

Life. From season to season, from generation to generation, from sea to shining sea and from continent to continent, it pulsates. A continuous, rolling, generative explosion, bursting all around us. Is this not the work of our Creator God?

You alone are the Lord.
You have made the heavens,
The heaven of heavens with all their host,
The earth and all that is on it,
The seas and all that is in them.
You give life to all of them
And the heavenly host bows down before You.

-- Nehemiah 9:6

If God is in all life emergent, the love energy that flows through all people and things, then God is our Creator. He conceives us, births us, and nurtures us. Which makes me wonder-- do we pay enough attention to the maternal nature of God? Perhaps it's time for us to widen our God-concept. For it is written: "God created man in His own image, in the image of God He created him; male and female He created them. God blessed them; and God said to them, "Be fruitful and multiply..." (Genesis 1: 27). Yes, God made all people-- women as well as men-- in His own image. Humanity in all its male / female complementarity is made by God, to be like God. God is fertile. God is plentiful. God is protective. God is ever-caring. These descriptions sound mother-like, don't they?

Once we sense gifts of motherhood as well as fatherhood in God, we begin to see a bigger, more complete Creator. As we do, we are not changing Him-- we are changing ourselves. As we probe the depths of God's love and care for all life, we begin to care more deeply too.

But God gave us free will. For too many decades, we humans have abused that freedom to plunder the planet. Nuclear powers have tumbled recklessly from hate to demonization to war. Too often, in our tribalism, in our embrace of autocrats, we have acted in ways that weaken democracy. Caught up in our small circles of care, too often we have failed to respond to the critical life-giving needs of so many around us. Given freedom, all too often we have done the small and selfish thing. How much different it would be if leaders of goodness all around the world were to ask each day, "What would Creator God do?"

Rising leader, you are our future. Your God-concept impacts your ethical formation. Will you look at the world as a mother would her children? Life is exploding all around you– look how bountiful, how threatened, how vulnerable, how worthy it all is. God has made us His creation's stewards. He calls out for leaders to rise up, to come to the aid of all life. To run to those in need. To save our world for our children's children's children. Are you ready to respond?

Next week, we will consider God's immanence– His presence in all people and things. And what it means for leadership.

"As a mother comforts her child, so will I, God, comfort you; and you will be comforted over Jerusalem."-- Isaiah 66:13

With love for life,

Tom

LETTERS TO RISING LEADERS

Week 3 -- Connected in Space

FRANCIS

Beneath the city lantern she stood fast,
clothes tattered, hair disheveled, face the same.
I handed her a Kind bar as I passed...
then turned and sputtered softly, "What's your name?"

With that, her eyes lit up with holy light.
"No one asks. I'm Francis-- like the Pope!"
It hit me how an act of mine so slight,
could impart in both of us new hope.

Perhaps this seems a weird way to explain
how we can stop temps rising by degree,
or how my race and your race might regain
respectful sense of shared humanity.

Perhaps systemic transformation starts
with one silent shifting of the heart?

Rising Leader,

The wider we open the doors of our hearts to God, the more we see
that He is in love not just with us, but with all people and things. I am
interwoven with the Great I AM– Who is interwoven with you– Who
is interwoven with all. Each one, each thing is a thread in the vast
divine tapestry called love. Once we see this, God's love-song calls us
deeper. His song begs a harmonic response from the bottom of our
souls.

Consciousness of our connectedness leads us to value the connections. We are naturally drawn to heal and strengthen them. We begin
to ask new questions. Is not the monarch butterfly good, worthy of
protection? Is not the valley stream that sparkles with cold, clear
water good, worthy of protection? Is not the Amazon good, worthy
of protection? Is not democracy good, worthy of protection? Is not

the Syrian refugee in a tent at the edge of Poland good, worthy of protection? Are you and your family not good, worthy of protection?

Yesterday morning, I took a walk in the woods. It was a new trail. As I ambled up and down the rolling hills, naked trees stood post around me. Something about the brisk winter on my cheeks, the beauty of the trees outlined against the sky, and the whispers of nature encouraged me to slow down. I began to hear distinct sounds of wildlife– rustles and scrambles and squawks. I began to step with care; the path was slippery (snow well-packed by those before me). I fell into a rhythm. And then something shifted. I became more alert. Aware. I awakened to the thought that I was just one presence amongst many, a contribution, one part of a larger whole. I was connected to the life and the beauty that surrounded me.

As I walked, I prayed. Not a vending machine-type prayer (put in the request, press the button and wait for the goods). It was more of an emptying prayer. A make-more-room-for-God prayer. It felt a lot like submission, surrender, allowing in, immersing with. By the time I stepped out of the trees, my soul was feeling in deeper communion with God.

God is immanent– Immanuel– God in us. He is the love-connection that binds all to all. Yes, *everything* emanates God's love. And everything is *alive*. The woods I walked through yesterday– the hills, the pond, the trees, the crows and squirrels– all were alive. A mountain is alive. Its rocks are made of atoms in continuous motion. From the atomic particle, to the leaping deer in the forest, to all humanity, to our planets and stars and everything in between, we are connected, with love interwoven. God in all.

But how do we connect with our Immanuel, in the midst of modern life? We are so preoccupied. Our screens have swallowed us up. Bottle-fed as we are each day by digital stimuli, we act like hamsters in a cage. Our attention falls into an ever-deeper deficit as we chase each shiny, new digital object. How easy it is to sleepwalk through life, to lead lives of quiet desperation. Never easier than now. It takes an act of the will to pull away, to seek out the holy.

And it is so important— especially for you, good leader. You must find the time; go to your quiet space. Only there can you find God. Once you do, you will see that He is with you intimate in your heart. You will begin to realize He was always with you and always will be– above, below, in front of, behind, beside and in you. As the psalmist says: "Where can I go from your Spirit? Where can I flee from your presence? If I go up to the heavens, you are there; if I make my bed in the depths, you are there." (Psalms 139:7-8).

Your awakening is of global significance, good leader. Our connected world staggers each day under a thousand cuts. Gifted leaders are needed if we are to weave back together the web of life rent asunder by humanity's greed and careless neglect. Yes, individual acts of goodness will help– but true transformation requires mobilization. Which takes capable, ethical leaders. This is why you are so import-ant, good leader. You hold humanity's future in your hands.

To be human is to go through desert experiences and periods of suf-fering. To be human is to someday die. Bad things happen to good people. But even then, even in the midst of all the world's hate, vio-lence, sickness, misfortune and pain, God is with us. And in God's redemptive grace, we can find the way forward– we can grow.

In these *Rising Leader Series* letters, I seek to offer you a path towards ethical leadership. Help on your soul journey. Like my path through the woods yesterday, your soul journey begins at the beginning, in an encounter with God. You don't need to look too far. He is in your heart already. Awaken to His presence, good leader. He loves you. He believes in you. He wants to radiate His love through you.

Next week, we will consider God's transcendence across time. It's a timely topic.

"The heavens are Yours, the earth also is Yours; the world and all it contains, You have founded them."-- Psalms 89:10

With hope,

Tom

LETTERS TO RISING LEADERS

Week 4 -- Connected in Time

THE GREAT I AM

Leader of promise, are you ready to start?
What premises, filters whittle your view?
What fuels your desire to serve from the heart?
What centers your universe: God or you?

God in windswept shore, monarch butterfly;
in every atom part, in galaxy;
in every cloud-borne droplet from the sky;
so too, your soul-- in all, divinity.

Bounding back before Big Bang's bombardment,
beyond sweet sequel to eternity,
behold in every right now moment:
God weaves you, with love, through time's tapestry.

Alpha, Omega! In you, me and all.
Great I AM whispers. Hear the quiet call?

Rising Leader,

In my last letter to you, I highlighted our connectedness in space-- to friend, to neighbor, to country-mate, to fellow human, and to all animate and inanimate things in the world– with God interwoven. God is aliveness, the luminous love energy we sense in all things. Present in every cell in our body, in all the atoms in the universe, and in the most secret place in our heart of hearts. This is what is meant when it is said God is "immanent".

But God is also *transcendent*, beyond the furthest boundaries of time. He is our Alpha and Omega-- the great I AM. God was, is and always will be. Before all of history. In this fleeting moment. Then on from here, into a thousand tomorrows and beyond– past all eternity. When we begin to sense God's connectedness across time, it causes us to care more about the future of humanity and its planet. God teaches us: tomorrow matters.

Remember the ladder I like to call the "disciplines of goodness"-- the one I've shared with you in earlier letters? All seven disciplines express care for tomorrow:

Sustainability
Diplomacy
Democracy
Charity
Civility
Decency
Piety

Piety is the foundational first step up the ladder of goodness. It is our journey from today into tomorrow– a walk we take with God by our side. Endowed at birth with original goodness and free will, we live to test boundaries. We make mistakes. We stray from God's steady stream of love. And then, perhaps when all else fails, we return to God. We open ourselves back up to Him. In such an encounter, God always begins with love. He transforms our fear (by love) into peace, and our remorse (by grace) into healing. As we begin to love ourselves again, we become ready to love others. This leads us to care, which leads us to act to advance the good. Piety gives hope and healing to our future– and the future of those we touch. In piety, we become pebbles of goodness dropped in the sea of God's love.

Our relationship with God makes us conscious of our interconnect-edness. We begin to sense the dignity of every human soul. We begin to live in a spirit of reciprocity. These shifts of the heart change how we interact. We begin to show simple human **decency** in everyday encounters.

The decency in our demeanor is sensed by others, making their days a little brighter– leaving ripples of goodness across time. Our decency brings to us an attitude of **civility**. We begin to show respect for all, especially those with whom we disagree. We smile, and people smile back. We listen, and people listen back. And so the ripples grow.

In civility, we become more conscious of the need around us– which leads us into acts of **charity**. We open doors to better futures for those we serve. Those who have received goodness soon seek to share it– love-ripples swelling higher.

Decency, civility and charity– all of these create the conditions for a healthier **democracy**. We commit to work within it to resolve our differences. We begin to see that what one side does in one election cycle impacts what the other side does in the next. So we compete within the guardrails, and work to strengthen the guardrails for the future. And so swells a rising wave of unity, flowing through our diversity. E pluribus unum– in many, one.

Emboldened by a strong democracy, we gain the moral clarity and credibility to advance ethical **diplomacy**. Diplomacy depends on trust, built up slowly over time, supported by many reciprocal acts large and small-- all connected in time. Blessed are the peacemakers who stir the winds of healing, washing whitecaps of goodness onto other shores.

With geopolitical stability and trust strengthened, it becomes possible for leaders in every nation to come together to advance the work to heal our planet. **Sustainability** is, in essence, lived-out love for future generations. Because we care about our children's children's children, we care for our planet. We rise to the challenge of saving and repairing it. We work towards a pay-it-forward, reciprocal world- - where what we take from the planet and what we give back to it come into balance. Until the waves of goodness have risen so high they have shifted the sands of time itself.

You're here for just a blink, good leader. What ripples will you make in the sea of God's love? I pray you will find, love and follow God– today and for all your tomorrows– so that the ripples of your life become a blessing to the world.

Next week, we'll have a chance to ponder the diversity of beliefs in our world, and what it means for Christian leaders.

"He has made everything beautiful in its time. He has also set eternity in the human heart; yet no one can fathom what God has done from beginning to end." -
-Ecclesiastes 3:11

Spend your days well,

Tom

Week 5 -- Pluralism

ROPE BRIDGE DANCING

Come join me on this bridge all snaggletooth--
ropes worn to thread, foot panels not all there.
Let's each come speak our deep authentic truth,
yet touch divergent ears with humble care.

As older, Christian, Minnesotan me;
younger, in-many-ways-different you;
not just to tribe will we speak honesty,
nor claim to be sole keepers of the true.

Out here upon this ragged common span,
shall we reach brave to offer up our hearts?
Authority, humility link hands,
while seek to crack blind certitude apart.

Can in my words to my own self be true,
whilst giving ear to your true self's truth too?

Rising Leader,

It's great to be back with you. I've thought about you often this past
week. I've prayed for you, too-- because you are our hope. You are
the one who will lead us with goodness in your heart.

Too often, the modern Christian message has been to pull away from
the world-- to shrink our circles of care-- to focus just on our own
private prayer and private morality. To affiliate just with those like us.
But this is not what Jesus teaches. Jesus Christ saw the connectedness
of all people and things, with love interwoven. He encountered and
served the marginalized, and ministered to the sick and the sinner. He
challenged the self-righteous. He stood up to unjust authority. He
saw no Jew nor Greek, nor Roman nor Samaritan-- just children of
God. And so He reached out to people of different faiths. As it was
back then, so it is to this day: Jesus calls His followers on an

ecumenical soul journey towards goodness. First to deepen our relationship with Him, then to widen our circles of care, and then to become His hands and feet in the world.

We live in a diverse world: 2.4 billion Christians, 1.9 billion Muslims, 1.2 billion Hindus, 1.1 billion secular / nonreligious / atheists, 500 million Buddhists, and 800 million devoted to other religions. We all share one planet; we are all companions, arms linked, on humanity's march of destiny.

I'm a Christian. Does my path to God enable me to claim superior goodness? Of course not. Each of us is shaped by our circumstance; each of us is free to choose our own path of belief; each of us is free to return to the good that is within us. We who are Christian have our own path, but that path calls upon us to reach out to all people. There can be no other way, in this pluralistic world of ours, if we are to take up the critical leadership work our age demands.

Pursuing goodness and exhibiting respect for others are central tenets in every faith tradition. Mature followers of all beliefs see goodness in all. Speaking in reference to all the world's belief systems, the theologian Brian McLaren differentiates faith before doubt- - which is about perfecting our set of beliefs-- from faith after doubt- - which is about moving beyond belief checklists into revolutionary love. What love is this? Abundant, indiscriminate love. Love for ourselves, for others around us, for all people (friend, foe, citizen, alien, the forgotten and the foreigner), for all living things, for the planet, for future generations. A mature Christian lives in mutuality with all-- called to "judge not, lest you be judged".

Fr. Richard Rohr refers to the world's major faiths as different rivers— each releasing mists into the atmosphere, which are gathered up into the clouds, commingling there with the waters of all rivers— a common spiritual love source. I am partial to Christianity as my path to God and goodness. Jesus Christ is my Lord and Savior, and I am forever grateful. But I will not condemn other pathways to goodness. On the contrary: I celebrate them. Goodness is of God, and goodness and Godliness can come from any human heart.

So how do we engage in constructive dialogue with people whose religious views are different from our own? How can we find common ground? How can we seek first to understand, then to be understood? This seems an important building block towards a better future.

Perhaps our whole approach to the human diversity around us has been all wrong. We tend to fly to the extremes. We either preach our truth in a tone that brooks no quarter for opposing views, or we bury our truth entirely-- sharing what we really believe only in the company of the convicted. But neither of these approaches works well. The first is tribal, judgmental, alienating. The second is inauthentic, untrusting of the capacity of others for tolerance, and noncontributory to the building of shared values.

There is a third way. Remember the "disciplines of goodness" ladder I shared with you last week?

If we work upward from the bottom, piety (our love of God, and God's love of us) teaches us the dignity of all. That leads us to become more decent and civil. And if we are ready to extend decency and civility to others, why not, then, speak our truth? With respect, we can offer our worldview as one lens through which our world's needs and challenges might be viewed. We can share why we believe this lens offers something important to the world. In this way, the teachings of our faith might be offered as pathways towards healing and renewal.

But to be life-giving, it must be two-way. We must also be willing to hear others share their truths. This interchange is not to be feared-- it's healthy. In the dialogue, our unconsidered beliefs are put to the test. We are challenged to ponder more deeply-- to self-reflect. It's so easy to float in a haze of lazy thinking and unquestioned habits. In back-and-forth dialogue, thinking sharpens. Habits are put under the light. Together, as we debate, we carve out a delicate three-dimensional sculpture called "shared values." And we begin to realize we are less different than we thought we were.

But of course we rarely do this. In our modern pluralistic society, we tend to avoid authentic dialogue. In private we cultivate our beliefs, but as we venture into the common square, most of us engage in sterilized happy-talk. Sure, a few come armed with a flamethrower-- especially in online forums. Vanilla or vitriolic-- nothing in between. Until elections come along, when all of our pathologically-suppressed convictions explode into volcanic conflict-- civility be damned.

I choose a different path. In my passion to support you in your mission to save the world, good leader, I write as a Christian. I care about the state of our world, I care about you as you rise to lead, and I care about God. I share my truth, because I believe it can offer you a path to lead in a way that can heal and renew the world. But I also respect other voices. I don't do this perfectly. But for those of good will who wish to contribute different voices, different perspectives, I say "welcome." Let's seek out harmony in joyful choir.

Authenticity-- that's the key. Let's talk politics, but with good will. Let's talk religion or nonbelief, but with good will. Let's celebrate Christmas, Easter, Diwali, Eid-Ul-Fitr, Hanukkah, Passover and Kwanzaa. Let's watch an indigenous dance, praising Mother Earth. Goodness calls to goodness, good leader. I encourage you: go out and connect with others of good will. Speak your truth, listen to the truth of others, find shared values, and encourage leaders of all pathways to come together in service of the common good.

Next week's letter will be filled with Spirit. Can't wait to share it with you.

"A new commandment I give to you, that you love one another: just as I have loved you, you also are to love one another." --John 13:34

Your Christian friend,

Tom

Song of the Month

FOOTSTEPS

Footsteps lead me to the woodlands
Close to home but far away
Here my heartbeat joins the choir
Of busy birds at the break of day

Timber falls as time intended
Pine trees rise cathedral spires
Spirit wind blows through the branches
Lifting hallelujahs high

CHORUS:

———

Holy Spirit
Search my soul
I've been unraveled
Come make me whole
In you I will authentic be
Come and set me free

———

Autumn ushers winds of changing
Oak trees, maples leaves of fire
Spirit blow my shut heart open
Fill me with renewed desire

Spirit God I've been ignoring
Things that now must be explored
Take these knots caught in the tangle
Work them free as you've done before

CHORUS

Holy Spirit linger longer
There's still so much work to do
As you whisper words of freedom

FIRST QUARTER: WHO IS GOD?

Help me make more room for you

Soon I'll step out of the forest
Nothing's changed but something's new
Soul and Spirit in communion
I see things now from a different view

CHORUS / Come and set me free

Search "Tom Mohr– Footsteps"
To find this song on YouTube, Spotify and all music platforms

LETTERS TO RISING LEADERS

Week 6 -- Leadership and the Holy Spirit

READY TO CONQUER

Thank You, Holy Spirit, for salvation
In You I cast off all of my reserve
You are my courage, strength, determination
I'm ready to be called; prepared to serve

This day will surely offer its surprises
Its twists and turns will be beyond control
But still, above them all Your Spirit rises
For You are now the captain of my soul

I fly on the wings of Your renewal
When I am down and troubled, You are there
You fill me with a holy fiery fuel
That lights in me an "I can do this" prayer

Boldly, bravely I will enter this day
Ready to conquer what e'er comes my way

Rising Leader,

If you ever visit San Francisco, try to make time for Coit Tower, at the top of Telegraph Hill. It offers a stunning view of the city, with the Golden Gate Bridge, the Bay Bridge and Alcatraz as backdrop. But a special visual gem hides within the tower itself. As you stroll around the inside hallway that encircles the building, you will find its walls adorned with expansive murals, painted in the thirties in primitive style by the artist Diego Rivera. These masterpieces evoke the beauty and struggle of daily life.

Here at the beginning of February, Coit Tower comes to mind as I ponder how to introduce the next few weeks' letters.

I feel what I've shared with you so far is much like Rivera's murals: big, expansive, not too detailed. The world is in crisis. There's an urgent need for capable, ethical leaders to rise up. Science offers great power, but it is ethically neutral-- it can be leveraged for good or ill. Which is why the ethical state of humanity's leaders is now so vital to our future. How to cultivate leader goodness? Goodness emerges from soul work. A centered soul will naturally rise to the seven "disciplines of goodness" that can save us: piety, decency, civility, charity, democracy, diplomacy and sustainability. It all starts with piety-- our relationship with God. As Christians, we conceive of God in three persons-- God the Father, God the Spirit, and God the Son. In the first four letters, we explored God the Father. This is the mural we've painted so far.

Yes, goodness emerges from piety. It is here we now need to go deeper-- to paint a more detailed picture. In the series introduction letter a few weeks ago, I promised to organize this series of letters broadly into four quarterly themes: "Who is God?", "Who am I?", "Where's the Need?" and "What's my Call?". All four of these themes touch on piety.

Over the past few weeks, I painted a Sistine Chapel picture of God the Father: God as supreme moral force, God as Creator, God as immanent (a luminous love energy humming within us and all things), God as transcendent (Alpha and Omega; beyond space and time). Today, and for the next three weeks, we will walk the next stage of our trinitarian journey. We'll journey with the Holy Spirit, as revealed in the symbols of fire, wind, water and oil. These are the four Biblical manifestations of the Holy Spirit.

Let's start with fire. Allow me to share a story.
A couple of years ago I joined a Christian ministry team on a weekend retreat inside a maximum-security prison. I was on the music team. Inside that prison, my job was to play music for twenty-two prisoners seeking healing for their souls. On the morning of day one, my teammates and I were led by guards past the gates, across Yard C and into the gym at the far end. As the retreatants began to stream in, I was ashamed to find both fear and prejudice rising in my throat. My stilted "hello" convicted me. I wasn't seeing these men. I was seeing "prisoner".

It left me troubled. As I picked up my guitar for the first song, the words pierced: "Amazing Grace, how sweet the sound that saved a wretch like me…" I realized it was I who was wretched: I needed that grace.

And then I began again. I really met, in the encountering sense, JoVon. Big. Darion. Harold. Blix. Pepe. Ron. Davide. I heard their stories. I felt their brokenness, their regrets, their yearning for forgiveness-- their yearning for God's love. I saw and shed tears. Come Sunday morning, as the sun played through a window high above me, the light displayed a cross-shadow on the wall. I felt the fire of the Holy Spirit surrounding it and me.

Yes, Spirit God came roaring in that weekend-- like a holy fire. As one retreatant shared on that last day, "My soul was parched like a dying plant, shriveled on the ground. But it's watered now. I'm growing in the sun again."

Right now, right in front of me as I write to you, I have on my desk the white baseball cap I wore on that retreat. Short notes are scribbled on it, in various magic marker colors: "Thank you for this life changing event in my life-- Big." "May God be with u 4ever-- Davide." "God is good all the time-- Blix." "May YOU stay 4eva Blessed!-- Pepe." "God bless you brother-- Ron." "Remember! If you inspire just one person to come to God, it's worth it.-- JoVon."

"Thank you for giving us your love!-- Harold."

It changed me. COVID came knocking the week after our retreat. The prisons were shut down. Within our ministry team I offered to initiate a monthly letter, written to all the retreatants-- my small continuing contribution to the work. I, a self-described leader, realized I was really just another sinner who needed grace-- just like the guys all around me. That insight freed me to become a leader again, a servant leader, in my own small way.

Rising leader, I mention this simply as one example of how, in our piety-- in our budding relationship with God-- we might discover Him in Spirit form, shining firelight so we can see our true selves. Imperfect though we are, He whispers to us: "You are loved. Just the way you are." And that changes us. As we welcome the fire of His love into our hearts, Spirit leads soul back to original goodness. The kind of goodness that can save humanity. For when Spirit fire touches our hearts, our goodness rises like a flame.

Leadership is expressed in a set of daily, practical actions. There is a right way to mobilize and optimize change. But change towards what end? For whom? With whom? The kind of leadership our world needs is *servant* leadership. It all comes down to your soul– to your goodness. That's the beginning of everything. And so, good leader, you are called to make a candle of your heart. Let Spirit God, by the fire of His love, set you alight from the inside out.

Next week, we will seek out the Holy Spirit in wind-- blowing change into our souls.

"If a brother or sister is without clothing and in need of daily food, and one of you says to them, 'Go in peace, be warmed and be filled,' yet you do not give them what is necessary for their body, what use is that? In the same way, faith also, if it has no works, is dead" -- James 2:15-17

In Spirit and fire, your pen pal...

Tom

Week 7 -- Holy Winds

WHAT FINE LEADERSHIP

Ironic what fine leader skills it took--
to mechanize destruction of our seas,
to slash for coal 'til Appalachia shook,
to make the Amazon more forest-free.

To capture darker passions at the polls,
to demonize the other in our midst,
to undermine those seeking common goals,
to counter outstretched hand with shaking fist.

Imagine what fine leaders it will take
to bridge delusions keeping us estranged,
to slow sweet sphere's slide with heavy brake,
to mobilize vast system counterchange.

O Spirit Breath from Whom all blessings flow,
Into starved lungs of servant leaders blow!

Rising Leader,

Today's world doesn't create much time or space for soul cultivation.
We spin around like perpetual motion machines, rarely slowed by a
reflective thought. From first awake moment to first drift into sleep,
we dog-paddle down an endless river of digital distractions: texts,
Facebook messages, TikTok posts, tweets, breaking news. Our
crowded calendars cause us to fly in a fluster from pillar to post. At
work, efficiency, productivity and pragmatism reign. If ever surprised
by a brief moment of downtime, cheap experiences lure. No church
on Sundays-- too many distractions. No morning prayer-- our phones
beckon with new nuggets of nothingness. And so we drift aimlessly
along-- floating away from the quiet, away from the sacred, away
from soul work, away from our true selves, away from the whispers
of Spirit God.

I myself have spent long periods of time caught up in that river. With ego distracted, my soul is left untended and unexplored. It grows covered in weeds and thorn bushes. Pathways through the tangles become ever more impassable. I become preoccupied, self-centered, trapped in obsessions, less capable of serving others.

It's not easy to get out of that river. Weekly church, daily prayer, solitary meditation? No community norms exist anymore to encourage these. It's on us to turn back to God. My return to the sacred begins when I sense a wisp of wind nudging me out of the current. A spark of honest reflection flickers. I become conscious of an emptiness, and I pay attention. And so it will be with you. As the wind blows harder, you'll begin to fight the current; you'll struggle towards the shore where Spirit God awaits. He meets you where you are:

> "In the same way the Spirit also helps our weakness; for we do not know how to pray as we should, but the Spirit Himself intercedes for us with groanings too deep for words."-- Romans 8:26

Time and again, the Holy Spirit has come to me in the symbol of wind. He came in a storm when I was twenty years old, as lightning struck me to the ground unconscious– a dramatic prompt to a big life reassessment. He appeared to me in a whisper on a faith retreat, softly saying, "I forgive you." He came to me as my father neared death, a light breeze of peace: "Do not worry. He is with Me." And he comes to me now in this moment as I write to you, in gentle breath, as my grateful lungs fill with the mystery of His love. Storm, whisper, breeze, breath– all are manifestations of the Spirit in wind.

Rising leader, can you open yourself to the Holy Spirit, coming to you in a storm, a whisper, a breeze, a breath? This can only happen if you create time for God. This is the first step in a life of piety. If you open yourself up, Spirit wind will blow into your life. With a gust, some weeds and thorn bushes may uproot and fly away, clearing your view. You will see your path as it twists and turns into the distance. With new eyes, you'll discover that it leads right back home, back to where you started, back to your original goodness, back to God.

Our time with God is important for our souls, but it's also a vital aspect of leadership formation. If we are to stay on the goodness path and not fall back into the river of distraction, we must welcome each new day as sacred. We must be reminded of our connectedness to all things and all people. In time spent together with God, alone and in a church community, we live the discipline of piety– and by doing so, we sanctify our day. We become open to metaphor. Soul and Spirit in communion, we feel the roar, hear the whispers, and sense the breath of everlasting Life within us. We become grateful. We begin to think of ourselves less, without thinking less of ourselves. In piety, day by day, blessing by blessing, we become ever more ready to lead in service of others.

Next week, let's refresh ourselves with a deep dive into cool, healing waters.

"The Spirit of God has made me, and the breath of the Almighty gives me life." - *- Job 33:4*

In encouragement,

Tom

LETTERS TO RISING LEADERS

Week 8 -- Healing Waters

LIVING WATER

To the well went woman fallen, filthy
Shackled, beaten down by the weight of sin
Shamed, she knew certain she wasn't worthy
Shunned, she boxed alone her shadows within

But Jesus came and saw the good within her
With love he sat, heard, dignified her worth
Then offered Spirit gift of living water,
to baptize her into a second birth

To this day Christ Jesus comes in Spirit
He meets us where we are, then makes us whole
He only asks a speck's first thought to seek Him;
with that His healing waters quench our souls

Spirit God, come shower my parched soul new!
And then, pray, show– how to love more like You?

Rising Leader,

Goodness and depth are intertwined. As long as we just swim on the surface, we will remain oblivious to the hidden motivations that impact our behavior– let alone the unresolved hurts and longings from which those motivations spring. To discover these, we need to dive into the depths, towards the bottom of the seas of our souls. Only then might we come upon pearls of wisdom hidden in the sand.

In my letters to you over the past two weeks, I have reflected upon the Holy Spirit, as experienced in the symbols of fire and wind. In fire, the Holy Spirit lights our path, warms our hearts and inspires our love. In wind, the Holy Spirit blows change through our souls, whispers guidance in our ears and breathes into our lungs the breath of everlasting life. Today, let's turn to a third symbol of the Holy Spirit: water.

Notice that these symbols are all metaphorical– all tactile. Fire warms us, ignites us. Wind cools us, awakens us. Water quenches us, cleanses us, refreshes us. It feels to me that there's something important here. When we begin to experience God in tactile ways– feeling the fire, sensing the breath of a whisper in our ears, immersing in the waters of His cleansing love– we reconnect with our aliveness. The lock on the gate of the soul clicks open.

I remember an experience in my mid-twenties. One week in early August, I joined up with five friends for a four-day canoe trip in Algonquin Provincial Park, well north of Toronto, Canada. We were all in similar situations, still finding our ways early in our careers. Underneath the surface, though, I was in turmoil. Still wounded by my mother's suicide when eight years old, I struggled with intense unresolved emotions. I had become an atheist in late high school (no loving God would allow mothers to take their own lives), and had carried that conviction through college. Shortly after graduation, after a knocked-to-the-ground encounter with a lightning strike, the first flicker of doubt had crept in, challenging my atheism. As I began this canoe trip, I still hovered in a no man's land between unbelief and belief.

For four days, with weather as our friend, we paddled and portaged from lake to lake following our map's scribbled path– a long, winding oval. Water was all around us, even when we camped. We drank from the lake. We swam. As we paddled, our paddle strokes mingled with the songs of nature– the splash of a fish, the twittering of birds, the wind in the trees when close to shore, and, once, the short-interval grunts of a moose unhappy with our presence. It was peaceful.

On our final day we started early, but by the time we completed the portage and shoved from shore on our last leg towards the outfitter's cabin where our cars were parked, the sun was riding low on the horizon. Five days in the woods had tuned our bodies to the physical. The lake was long, the night was warm, the water was glass. All was still; my heartbeat slowed. Our three canoes all fell into a synchronicity: ripple, ripple, ripple went our paddles, joined in perfect cadence. As the sun tumbled from gold to bronze to crimson against the treeline, as the water began to shimmer a thousand rubies and yellow diamonds, my shut soul creaked open. I began to sense a connection to something deep and eternal– something spiritual– something that felt a lot like love.

The change in me was not instant. My journey back to God was a winding one, taking years. In a sense I'm still on that journey, even to this day. But gliding along the waters of Algonquin Park that silent night, I first sensed the Holy Spirit, though I wouldn't have been able to name Him at the time– healing me, quenching in me a thirst I hadn't even known I had. He wanted me to know my mother was OK, and that I was loved. It wasn't long after that trip that, for the first time in years, I walked back into a church.

What I mean to say is this: we don't find God through some rational, intellectual exercise. It is an experiential encounter. It's tactile, metaphorical, mystical. This can be difficult for leaders, so conditioned to the rational, the analytical, the quantifiable. But God's first touch is on our hearts. Reborn into original goodness, we become more capable of sharing that goodness with others. And so we go back into the world. We find companions, we paddle along together, until suddenly there comes that magical moment when we ourselves are called to share with another the living water of our tears. By this path we become ushers for the Holy Spirit.

We can only find our center point and become more wholly present to others if we first confront our own hurts, regrets, longings, sinful patterns, hopes and fears. Will you welcome the Holy Spirit in, so He may shower you in the waters of rebirth?

For the past three weeks, we have encountered the Holy Spirit in fire, wind and water. Next week, we will find Him in oil.

"And hope does not put us to shame, because God's love has been poured into our hearts through the Holy Spirit who has been given to us."-- Romans 5:5

Wishing you much inspiration!

Tom

LETTERS TO RISING LEADERS

Week 9 -- Spirit Oil

ANOINTING

Will you find space for anointing Spirit
to love you, guide you, help you to be brave?
By other paths, hap you might achieve it--
for me there's just one path from self to saved.

Check: see if lurks some anger, bias, fears.
Might self-centered tendencies unglue?
It takes soul work to lead in sweat, laughs, tears
in acts of wisdom, love and justice true!

Do you desire to seize the servant mandate?
How equipped your shadows to engage?
How purified your soul to advocate?
How purposed is your heart to take the stage?

May Spirit God's fire turn your shadows alight.
Let Him banish darkness. Let Him sharpen sight!

Rising Leader,

By now, it's my hope that you see the links in the chain beginning to form. To put humanity back on a healing path, the world needs capable, ethical leaders. Given today's vast technical capabilities to advance good or ill, leader goodness is more consequential than ever before. Leader goodness depends on piety– strengthening your relationship with God.

The Christian path to God is the trinitarian path: we experience God in three persons. God the Father– supreme moral force, immanent in all things, transcendent beyond space and time– the Source of love. God the Son– Jesus Christ our brother, our Messiah– the Word of love. And God the Holy Spirit– the Spirit of love. Three in one, in mystical communion.

For the past three weeks we have explored fire, wind and water– the first three of the four symbols of the Holy Spirit. Now we turn to the fourth symbol– oil. God anoints us with the oil of belief, the oil of healing and the oil of leadership consecration. And then He shares His holy oil as fuel for our holy fire, igniting us with love, lighting our journey, and so completing the circle.

I admit that, for me at least, embracing this fourth symbol of the Holy Spirit requires a bigger leap of faith than does fire, wind and water. I didn't grow up having ointment placed on my forehead. Not until I fell in love with and married an Irish Catholic, and became one (Catholic, not Irish). But as I ponder it more, I see how the metaphor of anointing conveys honor and respect. The Bible tells us that God anoints us. And that blows my mind. How can it be that the God of all creation would stoop to honor and respect me so, especially in such a tangible way? It is I who am called to honor and respect Him. What kind of love is this?

And yet we learn that Spirit God does indeed anoint us in the oil of belief:

> "And it is God who establishes us with you in Christ, and has anointed us, and who has also put his seal on us and given us his Spirit in our hearts as a guarantee."-- 2 Corinthians 1:21-22

God doesn't push. He gives us the choice to let Him anoint us in faith. The rational brain clamors: "show me a sign– only then will I believe!" But God doesn't work that way. We are given our own free will, to see or not see– to trust or not trust.

Spirit God also anoints us in the oil of healing:

> "And they were casting out many demons and were anointing with oil many sick people and healing them."-- Mark 6:13

> "Is anyone among you sick? Then he must call for the elders of the church and they are to pray over him, anointing him

with oil in the name of the Lord"-- James 5:14

Whether it be our physical ailments or the demons that lurk in our souls, we all need healing. Holy Spirit God stands ready to anoint our wounds with healing balm. And so we come to Him, acknowledging our need, and accepting the support of our community. We let the "elders of the church" pray and anoint, in the name of the Lord. To take this step, to admit our woundedness, is an act of humility. Are we ready to become poor in spirit, so that we may be anointed?

The Bible also says that Spirit God anoints us in our roles as leaders, so that our leadership itself is consecrated in goodness:

> "You shall anoint Aaron and his sons, and consecrate them, that they may minister as priests to Me."-- Exodus 30:30

> "Then Samuel took the horn of oil and anointed him in the midst of his brothers; and the Spirit of the Lord came mightily upon David from that day forward."-- 1 Samuel 16:13

Leadership is fraught with risk. Far too many leaders succumb to power's addictions—such as pride, greed, envy and gluttony. It takes hard, courageous and continuous soul work to become a true servant leader. Where to start? The third step in the Alcoholics Anonymous twelve-step program is to surrender yourself to a higher power-- to the God of your own understanding. A quite successful person I know and love who is in recovery begins each day by falling to his knees in prayer, asking for the strength to remain sober today. We all would be well advised to do the same. As long as our pride-filled ego seeks independence from God, we deny ourselves His anointing oil. Only in kneeling surrender may we be consecrated.

And then Spirit God gives us oil to light our holy fire:

> "You are the light of the world. A town built on a hill cannot be hidden. Neither do people light a lamp and put it under a bowl. Instead, they put it on its stand, and it gives light to everyone in the house. In the same way, let your light shine

before others, that they may see your good deeds and glorify your Father in heaven."-- Matthew 5:14-16

Let us make our hearts ready, like wicks moist with holy oil, to be lit by the fire of God's love. This oil-fueled flicker of flame completes the Spirit circle (fire, then wind, then water, then oil, then fire). Anointed in belief, healing and consecration; lit up by fire; we are made ready by Spirit God to go out into the world and serve.

Next week, I will share some soul lessons taught by the most important person in my life: Jesus.

"But the fruit of the Spirit is love, joy, peace, patience, kindness, goodness, faithfulness, gentleness, self-control; against such things there is no law."-- Galatians 5:22-23

With prayers for you,

Tom

Song of the Month

I LOVE YOU MORE

The crowd gathered all 'round the hilltop
To listen to Jesus proclaim
Blessed are the poor in spirit
And the sad and the meek and the blamed
They shouted to Jesus "We love you"
And he smiled and looked back at them
For a moment he waited in silence
Then this is what he said:

CHORUS:
—--

I love you more
More than you'll ever know
As far as love can go
I love you more
Nothing you do
Can take me away from you
Just turn and I'm there for you
Just knock on the door
—--

The twelve gathered 'round him by firelight
Overwhelmed by the things he had done
They jostled to stand right beside him
To be close to the Holy One
With joy they said "Jesus we love you!
We'll follow wherever you lead"
Jesus looked to the stars in silence
And this is what he said:

CHORUS

The crowd gathered 'round Pontius Pilate
Who stood with a man at his side

"I can let this man go, he's done nothing."
But the crowd shouted back, "Crucify!"
They shouted again, "Crucify him!"
So they took him to hang on the cross
And just a handful of followers were with him
When dying he said to us all:

CHORUS

Search "Tom Mohr– I Love You More"

To find this song on YouTube, Spotify and all music platforms

Week 10 -- The Jesus Journey

EVERYTHING OR NIL

Across the globe hearts strive to lead lives worthy:
Muslims, Buddhists, Hindus, agnostics, Jews.
Christians, too, like me-- each of us searching
to live in sync with creeds we each hold true.

I offer you my Christian perspective.
But first I honor searchers everywhere,
who dive past the cozy, unreflective
towards depth-- while dodge dogmatic, doctrinaire.

For we who claim Christ's creed, our task is simple.
Jesus is either everything or nil.
Not just trappings, superficial prattle;
we're either Jesus-changed or soul-stuck-still.

For me, at least, Jesus is love, truth, grace.
Step you into His cross-crushed-hand embrace?

Rising Leader,

For the past two months, we have been wrestling with an important question: "Who is God?"

Our approach has been trinitarian. In January, we explored God the Father. In February we turned to God the Holy Spirit. Now in March, as we begin the "march" towards Easter, it's time to turn to God the Son-- Jesus Christ.

When, in His infinite wisdom, God chose to reveal Himself in human form, He could have descended as conquering king, in the prime of adulthood, in robes resplendent, with the heavenly choirs heralding His arrival. But that's not how He came. Conceived to a teenaged, unwed mother, He came into the world bloody, naked and weak. Born in a lowly barn, His first crib was a cow trough, attended by a frightened mother and bewildered adoptive father. Thirty-three years later, the Savior of the world would die as He was born– bloody, naked and weak.

What can we take from the fact that the great I AM, the Alpha and the Omega, Almighty God on High, Creator of Heaven and Earth, entered humanity on the bottom rung? Stripped of any trace of majesty or glory, He came to us (in the words of Mother Teresa) in the "distressing disguise" of poverty and weakness. As He entered adulthood and began His ministry, He sought out the poor, the homeless, the prisoner– to the point of becoming the same. It seems to me that this offers a powerful lesson in servant leadership. From the moment He was born, to His death on the cross, to His rising and ascent into Heaven, Jesus continuously gave away His power. God (in the form of Jesus Christ) always found the greatest need, and then descended right down to it. He preached what he practiced:

> "And sitting down, He called the twelve and said to them, 'If anyone wants to be first, he shall be last of all and servant of all.'"-- Mark 9:35

Piety lived out solely in private prayer and religious ritual is a hollow piety. Far too often, we keep "our faith" and "the world" separate. But Jesus shows us that faith comes to life in the world. The Christian way of surrender is the descending path– towards the bottom, the edges, the suffering. Prayer and ritual are good inasmuch as they draw us towards God, and towards a full Christian life of service to others in need. "What Would Jesus Do?" This is the Christian's most important question– how to live, as Jesus did, in the knots and tangles of life; how to serve the need in front of us.

In Jesus' teachings; in His use of time; in His relationships with the powerless and powerful; in the interrelationship between God the Son, God the Father and God the Holy Spirit we can discover many layers of meaning. Over the next three letters I will explore just three attributes of Jesus: His love, His truth and His grace. These alone are a good beginning.

What's love got to do with it? Find out next week.

"Thomas said to him, 'Lord, we don't know where you are going, so how can we know the way?' Jesus answered, 'I am the way and the truth and the life. No one comes to the Father except through me.'" --John 14:6

Blessings on the journey!

Tom

Week 11 -- The Love Way

LOVE EVERLASTING

Simon Peter, fisher. Be disciple!
Go away, Peter cried. I'm gripped in sin!
Follow me, beloved-- fish for people!
Lord, I am weak! Yet you call; I am in.

Vowed Peter: Where you lead, I will follow!
No, good Peter, three times you will deny.
So it was: thrice grilled, said, Him? I don't know.
Then fled from it all-- cross, death, tomb, the rise.

Until saw Christ risen. Cried out: I failed!
Yet Peter, my rock, on you my church builds.
He served Christ-aglow; proclaimed 'til was jailed.
And then on cross– feet up, head down– was killed.

Loved past failure, an up-down Saint stood tall.
Just so, Christ-love offers hope for us all!

Rising Leader,

Love Himself sent His only Son into our messy midst– to walk with us, to touch us, to love us, to forgive us, to die for us. He didn't come to condemn; He came to save. And he still does, every day. What love is this? It is Christ Himself: the universal, infinite, indestructible song that sings ever softly in our souls. The Bible tells us that nothing– not tribulation, distress, persecution, famine, nakedness, danger, sword, rulers, angels, height, depth, present, future, powers, principalities– *nothing* can separate us from God's love.

Except for one thing: ourselves!

Out of His abundant love, God gave us not only (in the words of Fr. Richard Rohr) universal free wireless, to connect with Him– but also free will. We can choose to connect, or not connect. It's our choice–

a choice of epic consequence.

Pride is the act of making ourselves our god. It is a forceful rejection of divine love; it separates us from God (and people). Leaders are especially vulnerable to pride. The more senior the leader, the greater the threat. It is why Jesus told us it's easier for a camel to get through the eye of a needle than for a rich man to enter the Kingdom of God. The power, the status, the money, the privileges– these all whisper that we are the special ones– above the huddled masses– worthy of homage– better than– self-sufficient. We walk into a room and expect attention. We go to a hotel and demand a room change if the toilet paper roll isn't spooled in the right direction. In pride, we place our egos on a golden pedestal, half expecting to be prayed to like a graven image.

Jesus lived love in its descending form. He reached out to the hurting, the shame-filled, the stuck, the fear-gripped. Even cowardly Peter, who denied Jesus three times after His arrest and then fled into hiding, was loved and forgiven– to the point that Jesus designated him leader of His church. Jesus loved the poor in spirit, those who mourn, the meek, the persecuted. Adulterers– prostitutes– tax cheats– prisoners– cowards– those who crucified Him– all of these He loved in word and deed. Even on the cross He cried, "God, forgive them. They know not what they do." Even on the cross He assured the repentant prisoner nailed beside him– "Today you will join me in paradise."

Jesus taught that love is humble, gentle, peaceful and merciful. It's patient and kind; it feels no envy; it isn't arrogant or irritable or obstinate or rude; it doesn't boast. It binds all together in perfect harmony. It accepts hardship, knowing that love always wins. Love is courageous– it overcomes fear. It requires surrender to receive it unearned, and then discipline to learn how to give it back to others. Especially we who are leaders must learn to let go of the seductions of the self, to open ourselves fully to God's love.

In this age of crisis, do you see how important love is to leadership? With love for God, our neighbors and ourselves, we expand our circles of care. We ensure the organizations we lead pursue goodness. Since we lead with love, we build cultures of respect and mutual support. We care about the person as well as the job. We see the dignity of others. We value authenticity and truth. We act with courage. In our community interactions, we act with decency, civility and charity. Piety, decency, civility and charity– these are the first four rungs on the "disciplines of goodness" ladder. All four spring from love.

Rising leader, built though you are to act, to conquer, to make change happen, I encourage you to pause. Jesus asks that you abide in His love, so His joy can be in you and your joy can be made full. "Abide"-- it's a wonderful word. In it we hear accents of surrender, submission, faith, hope, waiting, endurance, trust, patience– a "sitting next to", much like a golden retriever might do at the feet of his master. When we abide, we allow Jesus' love in and let it intermingle with our own love for Him. Surprised by joy, we sense a yearning to serve. And so we pray: "Here I am, Lord. I have come to do your will." A joy-filled leader is a wonderful sight to behold.

Next week, let's explore how Jesus integrates love with truth.

"No, in all these things we are more than conquerors through him who loved us. For I am sure that neither death nor life, nor angels nor rulers, nor things present nor things to come, nor powers, nor height nor depth, nor anything else in all creation, will be able to separate us from the love of God in Christ Jesus our Lord."- - Romans 8: 37-39

In loving fellowship,

Tom

LETTERS TO RISING LEADERS

Week 12 -- Truth Telling

FIRST LOVE, THEN TRUTH

The tax collect cheat, Zacchaeus the short,
Caught sight of visitor, crowd forming 'round.
Up tree he scampered to see, hear, report;
then something observed seized... struck him spellbound.

Jesus (the visitor) called as He passed:
"Zacchaeus, come here! Together let's dine."
In scrambling down to prep the repast,
Corrupt civil servant met Love Divine.

They met by the tree, then met eye to eye,
then met at the knock of his soul's closed door.
"I'm a cheat!" he blurted. "I stole!" he cried.
"To each defrauded I'll return– times four!"

Praise the change that befalls when, gripped in sin,
Final we stoop to let Christ's love-truth in.

Rising Leader,

At eight years old, on the morning of my mother's suicide, after my father had sat me down on the couch to shatter my world, while our church minister and a couple of police officers shuffled around talking to Dad in our living room, I gathered my six-year old sister and four-year old brother together. I found my little Bible, not much larger than a wallet, and opened it up, and just started to read. We were all crying. It was one of my last acts of unquestioned faith for fifteen years.

I grew up. I carried around a dark shadow of anger and guilt. Could I have been a better child? Would that have made a difference? Three years after Mom's death, Dad remarried. I became part of a Brady Bunch family, three joining three: a new Mom; a sister nine days older than me; two brothers two months apart; two Debbie's in the family. Wounded soldiers we were. Against all odds we emerged into a genuinely loving family– and are still one to this day.

As I headed off into adulthood, I was nonetheless weighed down by a lot of unresolved baggage. Mom's years of rising mental illness and eventual death continued to carom across time like a tumbling boulder, slamming and slamming into the tender parts of my soul. As a preteen, teenager and young adult, I acted out. I was selfish, and in that selfishness hurt others. I didn't let anyone get close to my heart. I chased experiences. I severed any connection with God.

And then in darkness, driving back home one evening through a torrential rainstorm to a post-college townhouse shared with friends outside of Miami, a feeling of great dread descended upon me. As I pulled into the parking lot and climbed out of my car, I was struck by a bolt of lightning. Literally. I came to, lying in a puddle of water, heart beating faster than a drumroll. The shock to my system scared me. Something dislodged. I realized I was lost. I realized I was in mourning– not just for my lost mother, but also for my lost God. This event was a truth moment– the starting point for a long, winding, multi-year journey back to Jesus.

Jesus comes to us first in love, but then in truth. We all have sinned. Obsessions and compulsions can all too easily take control of the steering wheel. As I said in my first letter to you, all people and things are connected, with love interwoven. We sin when we violate those connections in one way or another. This puts us into a soul-tangle, like a fly caught in a spiderweb, there to remain until we come to terms with what we have done. When at long last we turn to Him, Jesus brings truth to us– or perhaps better said, He brings us to the truth. He reaches out and takes our hand, offers a reassuring smile, and leads us into the dark shadows of our souls– there to confront that hidden truth. Only once we confront our sins can we descend into the humility of sorrow so necessary for healing. We fall to our knees, we suffer through tears of shame and regret, and then we look up. There before us stands Jesus, the One who was always there and who always will be, eyes shimmering with love.

Life with Jesus is a journey back to our original goodness. He teaches, footstep by footstep. He calls us from depth to depth– first to confront our big sin boulders, but then to detect and address the less obvious rocks and pebbles– the patterns of self-centeredness, prejudice and pride that lurk in our souls. He teaches us not to fear the truth, but rather to acknowledge it– while still loving ourselves. It's humbling to face our transgressions. Humility is good, insofar as it is paired with self-love. We get there when we remember that Jesus loves us with a passion beyond understanding, just as we are. He went to the cross to prove it. Knowing we are loved that much by Jesus helps us love ourselves. And so Jesus carries us forward, from love through truth to grace.

Rising leader, you are called to live in authenticity and truth. Your followers deserve no less. It takes courage to see things as they really are. Lao Tzu once said, "Truth lies waiting for eyes unclouded by longing." In your daily time with Jesus, you chip away at the longings and self-made walls that separate you from truth. Jesus puts you in touch with yourself first, and then with others. The more in touch you are with yourself– with your tendencies towards sin, with the tender spots in your soul, with your attitudes and even biases– the more capable you are of self-regulating, apologizing, forgiving and course-correcting.

Next week, we will ponder the awesome gift of Jesus' grace.

"Then he called the crowd to him along with his disciples and said: 'Whoever wants to be my disciple must deny themselves and take up their cross and follow me.'" --Mark 8:34

Yours in servant leadership,

Tom

Week 13 -- Jesus' Grace

SINNER SAUL TO SAINT PAUL

With hate harbored for people of the Way,
Saul hunted for converts to catch mid-flight
To Damascus road he went to snatch strays,
but on that road 'twas he struck blind by light

Why persecute? a Heaven-sent voice cracked
Who are you? blinded Saul, in fear, replied
I am Jesus Christ, whose church you've attacked
At Your feet I fall! repentant Saul cried

Paul is now your name. Go take up My cross!
With that scales cracked, clattered down from his eyes
He rushed to the margins to recover the lost
To his death he served; young church to make rise

Through grace, Christ made servant lead of St. Paul
Perhaps by grace we'll be made servant leads all?

Rising Leader,

In Jesus, God pierced the veil between Heaven and Earth. To
recover lost humanity, God took on human form. He became immanent – Immanuel– the Word made flesh. Son of the Living God, He
ministered to the marginalized, healed the hurting and forgave the
repentant. But He didn't just come to save those He happened to
encounter during His three years of active ministry. On the cross, our
Savior atoned for the sins of all humanity, across all time: "God forgive them. They know not what they do." This gift of grace is of
supreme significance to all of human existence.

Yes, Jesus descended to the margins to heal the broken. And He continues to do so every day. Jesus is the Universal Christ. He descends
right into our brokenness and weakness– if we let Him– and so saves
us from ourselves. The Good Shepherd walks into the valleys of our

59

suffering and dark caves of our sin to seek out our original goodness, much as a shepherd would seek out a lost sheep. He comes in love, then shines light on the truth we must know. At the first flicker of our remorse, He runs to us in mercy and washes our sin away in the waters of His grace.

Grace. It's God's most precious gift to the human heart. No sin can exceed the reach of God's grace. It is our passageway to renewal– to goodness– to service.

What part do we play on this healing journey? First, it's on us to open ourselves to Jesus' love. Swept up in pride, we might see no need for God. It may take a shock to the system to break us out of a pride trap. Or we may be swept up in despair. We might believe we are not worthy of God. It may require a slight lift of our heads– a glimpse up from the bottom of the well into which we've fallen, so that we can see the prick of light and the rope Jesus has thrown to us. Whether it be from pride or despair, God waits upon our first free-will movement towards Him.

But with our first turn towards Him, Jesus rushes in. He takes us by the hand and walks right into our souls with us, there to shower us with His love, truth and grace. Step by step He calls us into ever deeper communion. We repent; He forgives the big boulders of our past sins. We may feel unforgivable; He works in our hearts to help us forgive ourselves. Once we finally begin to forgive ourselves, He calls us to make amends.

And that's just the beginning. Then He calls us deeper. What harmful patterns lie beneath our sins? Do we carry within our souls certain prejudices, compulsions and obsessions? "Name these," He says, "and repent." As we do, He helps us to seek out and discover the hurts that lie at the root. He challenges us to look honestly at our human urges– to survive and procreate; for physiological comfort; safety and security; love and belonging; status and esteem. Have we properly integrated these urges of the self with the needs of others? Have we brought our souls into balance and reciprocity, tending to our own needs and the needs of others in healthy ways? Are we ready to widen our circle of care?

And so the dance goes on. Life experiences happen; our imperfections reveal themselves. Through our daily prayers we come back into communion with Jesus. Together with Him, one by one, we tease free the tangles in our souls.

For leaders, the danger of pride always lurks. In my first letter to you, rising leader, I said that all things are connected, with love interwoven. God is in all things– including in us. When we recognize that (and plug into the life force that is Jesus Christ) He leads us on a never-ending journey of healing, rebalancing, and renewal. The love, truth and grace of Jesus Christ are available to us each time we put our palms together in prayer. In the daily discipline of piety, we find the way, the truth and the life that sets us free. It is He who leads us to the truth, keeping us humble. Humility is a precious asset for a rising leader. Jesus points us towards the descending path, showing us the need, and inviting us to respond– with love, truth and grace.

Today's letter to you is the final one for the first quarter. For the past thirteen weeks, we have explored the question, "Who is God?". Starting next week, for thirteen weeks, we will explore: "Who am I?" What soul work do we need to do to become more whole, capable, ethical and selfless?

"You know the generous grace of our Lord Jesus Christ. Though he was rich, yet for your sakes he became poor, so that by his poverty he could make you rich."-- 2 Corinthians 8:9

See you next week!

Tom

LETTERS TO RISING LEADERS

SECOND QUARTER:
Who am I?

LETTERS TO RISING LEADERS

.

Week 14 -- The Sinner

HEY, GOD

Hey, God, I'm pretty sure You don't know me
I've kept away from You as best I can
Some folks say no sinner's beyond Your mercy
But actually, I'm pretty sure I am

You see, I have an angry disposition
Things happened that I simply can't forgive
Acts done in anger point me to perdition
Mistakes that simply cannot be outlived

So I don't know why I'm turning to You now
I really don't know who You are at all
But speaking my truth feels good anyhow
Like slowly knocking down a high brick wall

I don't trust, and don't know what You're about.
But I'm in sin. Will You show me the way out?

Rising Leader,

If there were to be a Sinner's Hall of Fame, John Newton would be in it.

Born of a mother who died young and a father who put him to sea at age 11, Newton was a reckless and disagreeable drunk in his youth. As he came of age, he took up work in the slave trade. As a seaman, his job was to chain and ferry Africans into slavery in America. Later, abandoned in West Africa by his fed-up crew mates, he was taken in as a hired hand by another enslaver. Only after his father sought the help of a sea captain to track him down did he make it out of Africa on a boat bound for England.

It was on that boat trip home that John Newton almost died. A terrific storm came up off the coast of Ireland, and the ship's hull cracked. As the boat began to sink, Newton prayed to God, pleading to be saved. At that moment, a wave hit the side of the ship, shifting the cargo in such a way that the hole was covered. The ship drifted to safety, saving all on board.

Newton didn't instantly become a model Christian. It took years before he finally renounced slavery. But his miraculous rescue from the clutches of death planted a seed. A period of deep self-reflection surely followed. As he looked inside his soul, he could not have liked what he saw. After becoming an Anglican priest at the age of 39, he wrote the song *Amazing Grace*: "Amazing grace, how sweet the sound that saved a wretch like me. I once was lost, but now I'm found. Was blind, but now I see." Later, he wrote an anti-slavery pamphlet, which received wide distribution and was delivered to every British member of Parliament. It fueled the push towards the eventual out- law of slavery in Britain.

From sinner to saved, from saved to servant— this was John New- ton's path. His journey of the soul began when he finally realized God loved him despite his sin. It continued as he let God guide him to the truth. In the bright light of truth, he must have fallen to his knees in repentance. And God forgave, as He always does. From there, John Newton began to forgive himself, until finally he was ready to step out of himself and embrace God's call to live out a new purpose.

Especially for leaders, it is so easy for us to drift away from goodness. Power is seductive. As Lord Acton, a nineteenth century British his- torian, once said: "Power corrupts. Absolute power corrupts abso- lutely." It takes serious soul work for a leader to counter these temptations. It's important work for all of us: the world needs capa- ble, ethical leaders.

And it all begins (and ends) with love. Each of us was born wrapped in God's love. At the moment of our conception in our mother's womb, we were endowed by God with original goodness. Then, as we grow from childhood to adulthood, we accumulate life experiences— many of them hurtful. These hurts ricochet inside our souls, wounding us emotionally. Our most sinful acts often spring from these past hurts.

But God understands. He has been with us, at our very side, through every bit of it. And He knows our every sin. Despite that, He loves us, just the way we are– while ceaselessly hoping that we will turn back to Him. Yes, He gives us free will to draw towards Him or push away from Him. But there is no doubt about His hope. He yearns for our return.

John Newton, a former enslaver, became a leader of great consequence. Newton's anti-slavery pamphlet made an important contribution to the banishment of slavery in Britain. *Amazing Grace* is still performed eleven million times per year. John Newton became a capable, ethical servant leader because he surrendered his heart to God. God led him, with love, through the painful dark valley of his truth to forgiveness– and then on to his calling.

As the Psalmist said,

> "I will be glad and rejoice in your unfailing love, for you have seen my troubles, and you care about the anguish of my soul" (Psalm 31:7)

Enough with the tribulations of the sinner. Next week let's turn our attention to the saint. But really, isn't it true that all who seek God and strive towards the good are, in the end, both?
"For by grace you have been saved through faith. And this is not your own doing; it is the gift of God, not a result of works, so that no one may boast."-- Ephesians 2:8-9

Your friend in God,

Tom

Song of the Month

BETWEEN THE MOMENTS

Between the moments
He was there at your first breath. He'll be there beyond your death
And if you stay for hours or days or months or even years away
From God he'll never go away from you

Between the moments
There will never be a time when God's not by your side
Turn to him

Between the moments of my life
Christ waits for me so silently, then reaches out to set me free
And in the moment of my strife
Christ's cross-crushed hand embraces me, a touch of peace that helps
me see
Between the moments

So many times I've been on my own
I've been in control, I have no need for him
Then suddenly life crashes in on me
And what do you see I'm out on a limb

Between the moments
He was there at your first breath. He'll be there beyond your death
And if you stay for hours or days or months or even years away
From God he'll never go away from you

Between the moments
There will never be a time when God's not by yours side
Turn to him

Search "Tom Mohr– Between the Moments"
To find this song on YouTube, Spotify and all music platforms

Week 15 -- The Saint

APPLES OF GOODNESS

Apples of goodness, ripe and in season
If plucked with pride could cast us from Eden
Warned C.S. Lewis: the greatest treason
Is to do the right thing for the wrong reason

So, as we rise, to our knees we must fall–
Lest puffer-fish egos swim self-enthralled
If we are to lead as creator God calls,
We must pray, pray again, preening airs to forestall

From God– our source of all gifts old and new
For God– our sole motive to carry it through
With God– our Guide who keeps our path true
To God– all glory for the good that we do

How to develop such fine self-restraint?
Commune with God– it's the way of the saint

Rising Leader,

On December 1, 1955, Rosa Parks was arrested for refusing to sit in
the back of a City of Montgomery, Alabama bus. A young pastor
from Dexter Avenue Baptist Church named Martin Luther King, Jr.
gathered up a small group of local civil rights leaders and mobilized a
boycott of the Montgomery city transit system. He was just
twenty-five years old: a young rising leader, just like you.

Blacks throughout the city stopped taking buses, which quickly thrust
the transit system into a financial crisis. King's home was dynamited.
His family's safety was threatened in other ways. But he didn't give
in. A year later, the city's buses were desegregated.

This was King's initial foray into the fight for racial justice, a fight that would shape the rest of his life. Building upon the success of this first protest, King started the Southern Christian Leadership Conference, composed of Christian civil rights activists from all across the South. He began to travel the country, discussing race-related issues with civil rights and religious leaders. Under the gaze of television cameras, he mobilized a protest movement committed to nonviolence, with sit-ins at lunch counters in Atlanta, boycotts and protest marches.

His commitment to nonviolence struck the conscience of Americans across the racial spectrum. What began as a small demonstration in one Southern city became a mass national movement. As police met protesters with attack dogs and firehoses, King and his fellow protestors responded with poise, grace and dignity. Arrested and put behind bars, he wrote from a Birmingham jail:

> "You may well ask: 'Why direct action? Why sit-ins, marches and so forth? Isn't negotiation a better path?' You are quite right in calling for negotiation. Indeed, this is the very purpose of direct action. Nonviolent direct action seeks to create such a crisis and foster such a tension that a community which has constantly refused to negotiate is forced to confront the issue."

In 1963, as part of the march to Washington, King stood in front of the Lincoln Memorial and gave one of the greatest speeches in human history. In his "I Have a Dream" speech, King spoke of the "fierce urgency of now." He foresaw a country in which all are treated as equals: "I have a dream that my four little children will one day live in a nation where they will not be judged by the color of their skin, but by the content of their character." His words and actions inspired and changed a nation.

Martin Luther King, Jr. was a saint, but he was not superhuman. In the months before he died, he gave voice to his work's toll: "I'm tired of marching. I'm tired of going to jail. Living every day under the threat of death, I feel discouraged every now and then and feel my work's in vain." And then he said this: "But then the Holy Spirit revives my soul."

Take note, good leader. King's relationship with God gave him the energy to keep going, despite the fear and suffering.

The differences between you and Martin Luther King, Jr. are fewer than you might imagine. When we idolize our heroes it makes it easy to distance ourselves from them. King saw and uniquely responded to "the fierce urgency of now." As you look at the state of today's world, do you not feel called to do the same? Yes, he was smart; so are you. He had leadership talent, just like you. He was afraid, just like you. King felt the fear— but he still moved forward. Will you?

It's clear where King's courage came from: his piety. King prayed and meditated daily. That's piety— the first step on the ladder I call the "disciplines of goodness":

The decency, civility and race-blind democracy he fought for flowed up naturally from the depths of his relationship with God. Rising leader, take the cue from Martin Luther King. Prayer and study are the wellspring of servant leadership. When you drink from that spring, you will fuel your desire to lead, and will refresh your soul for the struggles ahead.

For the past two weeks we've considered the archetype of "sinner" and "saint." Next week, let's consider the "sojourner"-- that solitary soul on a lonesome journey towards deeper awareness.

"A voice is calling, 'Clear the way for the Lord in the wilderness; make smooth in

the desert a highway for our God. Let every valley be lifted up, and every moun-tain and hill be made low; and let the rough ground become a plain, and the rug-ged terrain a broad valley; then the glory of the Lord will be revealed, and all flesh will see it together; for the mouth of the Lord has spoken."-- Isaiah 40:3-5

With thanksgiving for your passion,

Tom

Week 16 -- The Sojourner

I TOOK TO THE ROAD

Though confusions, compulsions cluttered my soul
I'd mastered contrivance to skip truth and such
With casual cast of my cloak of control,
I could cover my conscious– keep it unclutched

But the utter fatigue of it won in the end
One tap: soul broke open, its demons to fly
A maelstrom of consequence blew 'round the bend
Broke my defenses with one loud battle cry

Surrender! Surrender... I said with a sigh
Then, emptied of ego, I took to the road
Questions I carried 'long sweet by and by–
With space, time and God to help me decode

'Til somehow my sojourn returned me renewed
More humble, more faithful, more wise and more true

Rising Leader,

In her autobiography, *The Long Loneliness*, Dorothy Day describes her long journey from radicalized non-believer, committed to class warfare, through a period of doubt and deep self-reflection, through a faith conversion, and on to a God-committed life in service of the poor and fighting for social justice.

As a young adult, Day became a union activist, suffragette and social agitator. A member of the Socialist Party and a labor journalist, all she knew and respected were communists and socialists. None believed in God. In the wake of a suffragette protest in Washington, DC, thrown in jail, Day went on a week-long hunger strike. Hungry, afraid and utterly alone, Day was suddenly struck by a deep yearning for God. She asked for a Bible. She read and she prayed. Inside that jail cell, Day bared her soul to God. And so began a long, multi-year sojourn through deep inner solitude towards the divine.

It was a lonely journey. All of her friends were committed atheists— they couldn't comprehend her decision to become baptized, to become Christian. They drifted away. Her new walk with God began to separate her from all she knew. She began to realize that only in solitude could she find her essence, rediscover her deepest truth, return to her original goodness. On December 8, 1932, Day's years of sojourning and prayer culminated in a desperate plea to God— that "some way would open up for me to use what talents I possess for my fellow workers, for the poor."

God answered her prayer.

Dorothy Day went on to become a capable, ethical leader. For the rest of her life, she lived with and served the poor. She lived like the poor, divesting herself of possessions. She fought peacefully for social justice. She co-founded the Catholic Worker Movement, creating houses of hospitality for families in need. More than just food and shelter, Day worked to build a loving community, anchored in God. She encouraged those she helped to help each other— to see their connectedness to others in similar plights, and to create true community. She encouraged in her charges a vibrant faith life. Day died in 1980; to this day many in the Catholic Church advocate for her canonization as a saint.

Day's "long loneliness"-- her sojourn— led her through inner turmoil to a new life of God-centered servant leadership. It seems ironic that to emerge as a selfless, other-oriented servant leader, one first needs to descend into the self— one's inner solitude. Yet it's an important truth: we can't get beyond ourselves until we go deep within ourselves. This is the sojourner's journey.

This journey is of great consequence for the next generation of leaders. The world needs leaders well-formed, ready to fend off the temptations of leadership, ready to stay on the path of truth. Anger— greed— pride— fear— all of these lurk in the shadows of our souls.

Leaders cannot attain the vital attributes of decency, civility and charity— nor courage, nor love, nor justice— without first suffering the hard apprenticeship of constructive solitude.

What a tragedy it is, the unconsidered life. The deepest dream of our hearts is not so much for a life of accomplishments as a life of meaning. But meaning can only be gleaned through struggle and suffering. It is only in the silence of our hearts (braced by the courage that flows from faithful surrender to God who abides with and in us) that we can leap past fear and denial to shine a light on our shadow sins and compulsions. Only then can we begin the work of untangling and transforming them.

A sojourner is one who summons the courage to embark on such a journey. The sojourner climbs through and beyond the false self towards deep, essential truths. The most essential truths of our soul take time and effort to prize out. Sojourners must first shoulder the yoke of important questions, much as a mother carries a baby in the womb. So too, the questions must gestate. Upon the birth of Jesus, it was said of Mother Mary: "But Mary treasured up all these things and pondered them in her heart."-- Luke 2:19 The sojourner ponders— patiently and humbly abiding as difficult truth forms into consciousness.

Sojourn, rising leader. Carry the questions. Ponder in your heart. At the appointed time, truth will burst forth in all its clarity and beauty and forgiveness, and so guide you forward on your path towards righteousness.

Just as the sojourner opens up the soul for God to enter in, the seeker walks with God in search of truth. Next week, we turn to the seeker.

"Sojourn in this land and I will be with you and bless you, for to you and to your descendants I will give all these lands, and I will establish the oath which I swore to your father Abraham."-- Genesis 26:3

Safe travels, good leader!

Tom

LETTERS TO RISING LEADERS

Week 17 -- The Seeker

THE ARMS OF YOUR BELONGING

I've wasted time on cheap and shallow pleasures
I've chased for years the trappings of success
I've sought to tilt the scales past equal measure
With neighbors, family, friends and all the rest

I've skated fast atop the glassy surface,
steered conversations far from subjects deep
I've triple-bolted doors to my subconscious
for fear my soul would leak out tattered, cheap

But now, dear Lord, I search for better answers
I seek to plumb the depths, to find the true
I seek to learn from all my second chances—
to fashion principles of life that flow from You

I seek because I burst with holy longing
To settle in the arms of Your belonging!

Rising Leader,

Our world needs leaders who are seekers. If you are a seeker, you resist settled certitude. You keep probing attitude and belief. You know that superficial experience is just the tip of the iceberg; there is a much deeper reality to be explored. You dive below in constant search for first principles and essential truths.

To seek is to admit there is much we do not yet know about ourselves and our place in the cosmos. The unexamined soul is disorganized; cluttered. One can only lead a principles-centered life if one first examines one's patterns and biases, sorting and discarding as required.

To avoid this seeker's journey is to live in a haze. Stuck on the surface, motivations and assumptions rest undisturbed and untested. It's all too easy to ignore anything that doesn't directly and immediately impact our lives. This disconnects us from the universal connectedness that is God. As we walk by in a rush, revelation hides in plain sight.

In our unreflective state, we might blithely deny God's existence– "fantasy." Perhaps our unreflective selves dismiss His importance– "irrelevant to my life." Perhaps we place our god idol on a shelf like a fire extinguisher, to be used only in an emergency ("God as magician"... "God as solution vending machine"... "God as therapist"). Or perhaps our image of God provokes fear within us and leads us to demonize ("God as harsh judge... God as tribal leader... God as purity code / rules / orthodoxy").

These narrow God characterizations miss His truth. As we inch towards a deeper awareness of God, we begin to notice how deeply His love is interwoven into everything and us. We begin to sense both His vastness and His intimacy. A seeker opens the soul's door to a transformative encounter with God.

C.S. Lewis was a seeker. Perhaps you know Lewis by his children's series *The Chronicles of Narnia*. Lewis also wrote some of the most important books on Christian apologetics of the twentieth century– including *Mere Christianity* and *The Problem of Pain*. But Lewis' journey to the pinnacle of Christian thought was by no means linear. In his teenage boarding school years, he utterly abandoned his childhood Christian faith. He'd become convinced he was doing prayer all wrong, and it tormented him. Being a Christian had begun to feel like an endless chore. When a teacher happened to share her passing fascination with the occult, Lewis became enthralled. He shed his Christian religion like a cheap suit. He soon began to intellectualize his desertion, embracing atheism-- well defended by materialism and rationalism.

But seeker that he was, he didn't stop there. A gifted student and talented writer, he consumed the classics. He embraced rhetoric and dialectic. Over time, Lewis built an impressive intellectual edifice of atheism. Awarded a scholarship to attend Oxford, he was well on his way towards perfecting this edifice when World War One intervened. Called to service, he fought in the trenches, saw the horrors of war, encountered fellow soldiers for whom God was paramount, and saw close friends die. After the war he returned to Oxford, eventually becoming a professor in the English Literature department.

Soon Lewis began to see chinks in atheism's armor. He couldn't shake a bothersome pattern. Widely read, he began to notice that many writers (such as Shaw, Wells, Voltaire and Mills) presented elegant rational thought frameworks utterly disconnected from the deeper reality he had sensed in the real-world experiences of life. On the other hand, other writers (including MacDonald, Chesterton, Milton and Tolkein) seemed to plumb the depths of that reality in ways that completely eluded the first group. How inconvenient it was to find that all in the first group were atheists; all in the second group were Christians.

For Lewis, a seeker, each plank in his platform of atheism needed to be put to the test. And so he listed the arguments of theists and atheists alike. He listened and advocated in equal measure, testing both sides of the debate. Soon, new chinks emerged. Plank by plank, frame by frame, Lewis' entire atheistic edifice eventually began to slip off its foundation. This was traumatic for him. As it all began to crack and tumble to the ground, he found himself hemmed in by one final, unavoidable conclusion– the one thing that still stood amidst the shattered remains of his former beliefs:

> "That which I greatly feared had at last come upon me. I gave in, and admitted that God was God, and knelt and prayed: perhaps, that night, the most dejected and reluctant convert in all England."

At first his only acknowledgement, a grudging one at that, was that God exists. It took another two years for Lewis to embrace Christianity. The final shift occurred on a long walk with J.R.R. Tolkein (author of the *Lord of the Rings* series), a fellow faculty member who had become a close friend. Tolkein, a devout Catholic Christian, said of Jesus: "Either this man was and is the Son of God, or else he is a liar, a lunatic or a fraud." No cozy middle ground was possible. Later on the walk Tolkein said, "The story of Christ is a myth, like all other myths, but with one tremendous difference– it really happened." At that moment, as Lewis described it, a rush of wind came up. He felt something shift, as if tumbles in a lock mechanism had finally slipped into place, causing a door to open. With that he walked into the light.

Lewis became a leader of great consequence. During World War Two, he hosted a radio hour during which he shared the Christian message with his war-besieged countrymen. These talks became the basis for his book *Mere Christianity*. Just as, to this day, *The Chronicles of Narnia* captivate generations of children (conveying to millions the deeply Christian themes embedded therein), his other books (especially *Mere Christianity*, *The Problem of Pain*, *The Screwtape Letters* and *Surprised by Joy*) have become staples for Christian seekers everywhere. His books have sold 200 million copies, and have been translated into 30 languages.

None of it would have happened had Lewis not been a seeker. He had the intellect and the courage to go deep– to find first principles– to find God. And that made all the difference.

May the road rise to meet you, good seeker! And may your search lead you towards service– which is the topic of next week's letter.

"Ask, and it will be given to you; seek, and you will find; knock, and it will be opened to you."-- Matthew 7:7

Your fellow seeker,

Tom

Week 18 -- The Servant

A GOOD LIFE

To college he went, then to rising career
Married, three kids, until tragedy struck
Widowed, he wondered: "Where do I go from here?
No Mom for the children-- me down on my luck"

But up from the depths he rose, brushed off the dirt
Opened his heart again, found wounded love
Three kids became six, each with gifts, joys and hurts
From chaos grew family, soul-touched from above

Each of Dad's children count dear to this day
The pure, saving grace of his soft, tender care
Is this servant leadership? It is, I say
Times six he gave all-- times six he love-shared

Great is the reach of a good leader's worth
When love meets child, neighbor, nation or Earth

Rising Leader,

It is the habit of our times to separate our world lives from our faith lives. But this is silliness. Our faith teaches us how to live our lives in the world-- how to see God in all people and things, and how to respond to His call. Given the challenges of our time, we need leaders who are both capable and ethical. How do leaders become ethical? You will recall (from previous letters) the ladder of virtues I call the "disciplines of goodness":

It all flows up from the bottom. Servant leadership begins in our souls, in our relationship with God. With God by our side, in prayer and contemplation, we work to untangle soul knots. Once set free from our self-preoccupations, we look beyond ourselves. We begin to see dignity in all people. We begin to see our interconnectedness. This frees us to move up the ladder: to become more decent, civil and charitable. As we come to recognize the equal worth of all people now and in future generations, we become committed to the advancement of democracy, diplomacy and sustainability. It all flows up.

In the life of Dag Hammarskjold, we find a servant leader who kept his world life and his faith life deeply integrated. Here is a man who spent his life working to steer a fractious world away from the abyss. We can learn much from his story.

Hammarskjold was elected Secretary General of the United Nations in 1953 at the age of 47 years old. He was the only prospect for the job that all parties– the Soviets, the Western nations, China, and the other nations of Asia and Africa– could agree on. His good will and unimpeachable integrity were visible to all.

It's hard to overstate the tenuous condition of geopolitics at the time. Just eight years had passed since the end of a war that had claimed 75 million lives. The United Nations had been formed to avoid another descent into the hell of global conflict. In the years leading up to the end of World War II and shortly thereafter, Europe had been cut in two by the Iron Curtain. It had experienced massive human displacement. Stalin held all of Eastern Europe in his grip. The West, fearing the spread of Communism, mobilized to block Soviet expansion. Post-occupation Japan and Germany were still in shambles, struggling to find a new way forward. Many Jews who had survived the Holocaust left Europe for Palestine. Soon they were fighting the British colonialists and native Palestinians to establish a new state of Israel. From Mahatma Gandhi in India to Messali Hadj in Algeria, new leaders were inspiring independence movements against colonial powers throughout Asia and Africa. Flash points were everywhere.

Time and time again on the global stage, Hammarskjold ran to the need and intervened personally to broker differences between competing parties. In his diplomatic work, he always sought first to understand. He once said, "You can only hope to find a lasting solution to a conflict if you have learned to see the other objectively, but, at the same time, to experience his difficulties subjectively." He invented shuttle diplomacy, which he used to great effect in diffusing the Suez crisis, rising tensions in the Middle East, and civil war in the Congo. It was in the Congo, en route to another diplomatic meeting, that his plane crashed (under mysterious circumstances) and he died. President John F. Kennedy called him "the greatest statesman of our century." To this day, Hammarskjold is the only person to have ever been posthumously awarded the Nobel Peace Prize.

How did Hammarskjold become such a capable, ethical servant leader? The answer lies in his interior faith journey. After he died, his personal journal was found in his New York apartment, containing his spiritual reflections. He had started the journal when twenty years old; its final entry was just a month before he died. Here in this journal, the entire arc of a global leader's private relationship with God was revealed. Published under the title *Markings*, it became a best-seller.

It was in this journal that the UN Secretary General bared his soul. "Before Thee, Father, in righteousness and humility. With Thee,

Brother, in faith and courage. In Thee, Spirit, in stillness. Thine, for Thy will is my destiny; dedicated, for my destiny is to be used and used up according to Thy will." Hammarskjold's journal reveals vigilance against the sin of pride. Writing about himself, he said, "You listen badly, and read even worse. Unless it's about yourself. Then you pay careful attention." He strived for daily renewal in his life of service: "Each day the first day. Each day a life. Each morning we must hold out the chalice of our being to receive, to carry, and give back. It must be held out empty — for the past must only be reflected in its polish, its shape, its capacity."

For Hammarskjold, the connection between God, soul work and his role as a servant leader was unbreakable. If we are to live out our Christian faith, it cannot begin and end in private prayer and private morality. To be most fully Christian is to study, to pray, to search out our sins, to seek forgiveness, to welcome God's grace, to deepen our sense of connectedness to God and all things, to form a conscience, to hear our call and then to go into the world and serve– animated by a gentleness of spirit. Dag Hammarskjold did just this, teaching us the way.

Our hurting world waits, good leader. Will you do the same with your life? If not you, then who?

Next week. we will begin a four-letter exploration of the dark night of the soul.

"Jesus called them together and said, 'You know that those who are regarded as rulers of the Gentiles lord it over them, and their high officials exercise authority over them. Not so with you. Instead, whoever wants to become great among you must be your servant, and whoever wants to be first must be slave of all.'"-- Mark 10:42-44

In service,

Tom

Song of the Month

STRUGGLE

One more time now, and you won't answer
One more prayer you won't listen to
One more try Lord, I am calling
One more night that I can't get through

REFRAIN:

And I really don't know why I'm even trying
To find your face and your embrace
I'm tired. I'm lonely. I'm angry
Can't you hear my prayer?
Try whispers. Try wonders. Try lightning
Are you even there?

Long ago, I thought I knew you
But where are you when all hope is gone?
Find me here in a place called nowhere
It's a dark, dark place when there's no hope of dawn

REFRAIN

BRIDGE:

Lord, I'm praying and I'm reading and I'm praying
And I'm seeing that you say you'll never leave me alone.
Lord I'm hurting, I'm still hurting but you're working
Yes I'm on my own, but maybe not alone

One more time now and you have answered
One more prayer that you've listened to
Once again Lord, you've come calling
One more night that you've helped me through.

And I really don't know how it ever happened
That I found your grace and your embrace
I'm tired. You're holy. You love me.
You have heard my cry.
You've whispered your wonder, I bend down.
You are God on High.

You are God
You are God
You are God On High

Search "Tom Mohr– Struggle"
To find this song on YouTube, Spotify and all music platforms

Week 19 -- Doubt

WILL THAT LIGHT

When a bottle, well hidden, proves worst fears
When a child's diagnosis hangs like rope
When a love-bond severs in twilight years
When a two-soldier knock shatters hope

When life as we know it is swept downstream
When time's endless promise sudden times out
When the stitch of our dreams splits at the seams
Certain's the stumble– the fall into doubt

Inside doubt's tunnel, so long, black as night
We wrestle with demons– wrestle with Him
Until at end of the tunnel, a light
Just a pin, then flicker– distant and dim

Behind: dark doubt beckons– and deeper, despair
Ahead: will that Light keep flickering there?

Rising Leader,

Starting this week and for the rest of this month, I will journey with you into the dark night of the soul: our moments of doubt, disconnection, disillusionment and despair. How can we continue to lead in the midst of darkness? How might our darkness be transformed, so as to strengthen our capacity to lead? We will take up these questions by pondering the struggles and triumphs of four capable, ethical leaders.

We begin with doubt.

If you have ever struggled with doubt, you are in good company. For twenty years, Mother Teresa taught at a convent school in Calcutta– until on September 10, 1946, traveling to an annual retreat by train, she saw a crucifix-- Jesus on the cross. She sensed Jesus saying to her: "I thirst". As she looked upon this icon of poverty and pain, something beckoned her towards a new vision for her life. Shortly thereafter she asked and received permission to depart the convent, so that she could go out into the world to serve the poorest of the poor.

With no possessions to her name, she went into the Calcutta slums and began to minister to the sick-- the abandoned ones, those waiting on the streets to die. It began when she bent down to care for just one. She helped that one-- and then found another, and another. Soon her gaze widened-- she took in the people living in poverty all around her. She began to internalize the hardships they faced. Writing in her diary, she said:

> "Our Lord wants me to be a free nun covered with the poverty of the cross. Today, I learned a good lesson. The poverty of the poor must be so hard for them. While looking for a home I walked and walked till my arms and legs ached. I thought: how much they must ache in body and soul, looking for a home, food and health."

At first, hers was a solitary street ministry. But her first small acts of kindness attracted others seeking to serve. Donations trickled in. In 1950 she founded the Missionaries of Charity. By the time of her death in 1997, 4,500 Mission of Charity nuns were working with the poorest of the poor in 133 countries around the world. In 1979, she received the Nobel Peace Prize; in 2016, Mother Teresa was canonized as a saint by the Catholic Church.

Mother Teresa was a servant leader of great consequence. For fifty years she carried the message of God's love, the truth of humanity's connectedness and passionate advocacy for the poor to listeners everywhere, all round the globe:

> "The fruit of silence is prayer; the fruit of prayer is faith; the fruit of faith is love; the fruit of love is service; the fruit of service is peace... Today, if we have no peace, it is because we have forgotten that we belong to each other-- that man, that woman, that child

is my brother or my sister. If everyone could see the image of God in his neighbor, do you think we would still need tanks and generals?... The poor must know we love them, that they are wanted. They themselves have nothing to give but love."

Given all she did for God, it is easy to imagine that Mother Teresa lived her life on some spiritual plateau unattainable by mere mortals, steeped in a continuous, intimate, shimmering love relationship with the divine. But the opposite was true. For 50 years she struggled in the desert, searching in vain for a sign that God remained by her side. She was besieged by doubt, writing privately:

"Lord, my God, who am I that You should forsake me? The Child of your Love– and now become as the most hated one– the one You have thrown away as unwanted– unloved. I call, I cling, I want– and there is no One to answer– no One on Whom I can cling– no, No One– Alone... Where is my Faith– even deep down right in there is nothing, but emptiness & darkness– my God– how painful is this unknown pain– I have no Faith– I dare not utter the words & thoughts that crowd my heart– & make me suffer untold agony."

It seemed that the more success Mother Teresa experienced in her work, the more empty her soul felt– the more she doubted God. She told her confessor:

"When I try to raise my thoughts to heaven, there is such convicting emptiness that those very thoughts return like sharp knives and hurt my very soul. I am told God loves me, and yet the reality of darkness and coldness and emptiness is so great, nothing touches my soul."

This shocks us. How could it be that the modern world's most recognized face of holiness could have been besieged, for 50 years, by unrelenting doubt? If such was her fate, what hope is there for the rest of us?

Doubt is a necessary and inevitable part of an authentic journey of faith. St. John of the Cross, the 16th century Spanish mystic, named it the "dark night of the soul". In the darkness of our doubt, we confront our greatest fear: that God has turned away from us— or worse, that he was never there at all.

For some, doubt comes in the wake of shattered hopes. For the young couple who has just learned their baby will be cognitively compromised for life; or for the woman who has just been fired from the only job she ever wanted; or for the recently-retired, sixty-five year old grandfather who has just learned he has terminal cancer— God can seem distant. In the midst of this doubt we are forced into a painful reassessment of who God is— and who He isn't. Sometimes God rescues us from trial; sometimes he accompanies us in love as we go through trial. And so we struggle with the nature of God. We cast off old notions. We grieve. The questions linger…

Why is there so much suffering in the world? Why do bad things happen to good people? Why, when we turn towards God, do we feel nothing? There are no easy answers to these questions. In the end, all we can do is to live with them— abide in them— wait at the foot of the Cross for clarity. It may come. It may not come. In the end, doubt presents us with a stark choice: to believe despite our unbelief, or to abandon our search for God entirely. Mother Teresa chose the first path. For 50 years doubt and trust quarreled in her soul. Though she never fully resolved this quarrel, she chose nonetheless to love and serve God and the poor until her dying breath— and because of that choice, she transformed the world. In the end we all must decide: can God's silence be trusted?

If doubt is a crisis of trust, disillusionment is a crisis of belief. This is the topic of next week's letter.

"Jesus asked the boy's father, 'How long has he been like this?' 'From childhood,' he answered. 'It has often thrown him into fire or water to kill him. But if you can do anything, take pity on us and help us.' 'If you can?' said Jesus. 'Everything is possible for one who believes.' Immediately the boy's father exclaimed, 'I do believe; help me overcome my unbelief!'-- Mark 9:21-24

In trust and belief,

Tom

Week 20 -- Disillusionment

WHY, GOD?

Ukrainian Alisa, nine years old,
Was scrambling with her family 'cross the bridge
Weighed down by pack and bundled 'gainst the cold
She began to lag behind just a smidge

As bombs rained down, inching ever closer
Mother's panicked lips began to pray
Young Mykyta slowed to help his sister
And took her by the hand to speed her way

But bombs are bombs: the family never made it
The world viewed fresh, dead bodies on the ground
Damn it, but God (may I be explicit?)
I'm haunted by the thought You weren't around

It's the part of faith I've ne'er understood
Why is it evil sometimes conquers good?

Rising Leader,

No matter what your peg is on the leadership pyramid, it is inevitable that some day, in some way, your ethics will be tested. For those privileged to reach the peak– especially in politics, business and science– powerful tools and resources will be at hand. As recent world events so vividly teach, the goodness of a leader is of paramount concern to all of us. Only leaders of goodness will use the tools and resources available to them for the good.

Where is the ethical foundation of a leader formed? In piety. Only when we enter into God's presence do we discover the audacity of His love for us. God reaches past the walls of our false selves to find the true. It is here we learn to move beyond ourselves; to expand our circles of care; to serve.

Our piety is formed in quiet prayer; in good times and bad; in the heat and shadows. To reach maturity in our faith, we must at times "walk through the valley of the shadow of death." In this letter, I wish to explore the shadow of disillusionment. Disillusionment is the dissolution of a belief we once thought to be true. The veil of false belief is ripped from our face, shocking us into a new awareness both troublesome and disorienting. The world as we once knew it no longer exists. Before us lies some new and uncomfortable reality. We grieve for what was; we resist– but can't deny– what is.

Perhaps our disillusionment is in God Himself, experienced when first we realize He will not give us the thing we so desperately seek. This forces us to reimagine who God is and isn't. We must choose anew whether to believe. Will this reimagining of who God is help us to rediscover His love for us? Or will it lead us to reject or deny Him? Perhaps we are disillusioned by those around us– we are surprised by their selfishness or greed or envy or even cruelty. Is it possible to accept but transcend this reality, to see it through God's eyes, and to find our way back to forgiveness and love? Or will our hurts descend into hates? Disillusionment provokes questions such as these.

Today I would like to share the story of Corrie Ten Boom. Corrie was the daughter of a watchmaker who lived in Amsterdam during World War II. She lived a simple, stable, happy life inside a loving family. In May of 1940, the Nazis invaded the Netherlands. Soon the occupying force mobilized to implement its "final solution"-- the extermination of the Jews. Realizing what was happening, Corrie's father asked the family to welcome Jews into their home. They built a secret hiding place behind a false wall, right in Corrie's own bedroom. For two years, Corrie, her sister Betsie and the Ten Boom family hid many Jews behind that wall, and then helped them to escape out of the country.

Eventually the Ten Booms were caught, betrayed by a neighbor. Corrie, Betsie and the rest of the family were thrown into prison. Corrie and Betsie ended up in the same concentration camp-- called Ravensbruck. Corrie was just 26 years old at the time. Imagine her disillusionment: betrayed by friends, stripped from her happy family, denied freedom, caught in the clutches of evil. All notions of the goodness of humankind, all trappings of home and promises for the future were shattered as the gates of Ravensbruck closed behind her.

Upon their arrival, she and her sister were stripped of their clothes— in front of the guards. They were given rough prison garb and thrown into a barracks, the sleeping platforms stacked three high, crawling with fleas and other prisoners. On that first night, they hud- dled together as Betsie began to pray. "Show us, God. Show us how". Betsie had somehow managed to smuggle into the prison a small Bible. She read from the book of Thessalonians. A phrase struck her, and she said to Corrie, "That's it. That's His answer. 'Give thanks in all circumstances!' That's what we can do. We can start right now to thank God for every single thing about this barracks!" And so they did. They even gave thanks for the fleas.

Corrie Ten Boom's time inside Ravensbruck was her dark night of the soul. In the terror of darkness, she encountered the crush of disil- lusionment. It took time, but through constant prayer she began to transcend it. She and her sister celebrated the fact that they had each other. They found solace in helping others. Armed with their small smuggled Bible, they organized a clandestine Bible study group. Cor- rie took on the role of visiting and encouraging others, saying prayers with them, and reading the Bible to them. She did all this right under the noses of the guards. Their Bible study group was never discov- ered. Corrie later learned she and her sister had been protected by the fleas: the guards avoided roaming the barracks for fear they them- selves would become infested.

Betsie died in Ravensbruck. Corrie survived. After the war, Corrie went on to share her story and her Christian faith to audiences all around the world, awakening the faith of many. A leader of good- ness, she traveled far into her old age, speaking to audiences large and small about the love of God and the power of forgiveness.

In 1947, at the end of such a talk in Munich, Corrie saw a man approaching her. She froze. She instantly knew that the man coming up the aisle towards her was a former Ravensbruck guard. In that moment, she later said, it was as if he still wore his visored cap with the skull and crossbones, the blue uniform, the leather crop swinging from his belt. With horror she recalled her naked walk past him, her clothes thrown on a huge pile on the floor along with those of other newly admitted prisoners.

He said, "I too was at Ravensbruck. Since then I have become a Christian. You say that God forgives all sins, and indeed I know God has forgiven me for all the cruel things I did there. But I hope to hear it from your lips as well. Will you forgive me?" Corrie Ten Boom knew her faith– the proof of her progress past disillusionment– was being tested.

Corrie described what happened next:

> It could not have been many seconds that he stood there, hand held out, but to me it seemed hours as I wrestled with the most difficult thing I had ever had to do. For I had to do it–I knew that. The message that God forgives has a prior condition: that we forgive those who have injured us. 'If you do not forgive men their trespasses,' Jesus says, 'neither will your Father in heaven forgive your trespasses.'... And still I stood there with the coldness clutching my heart. But forgiveness is not an emotion–I knew that too. Forgiveness is an act of the will, and the will can function regardless of the temperature of the heart. 'Jesus, help me!' I prayed silently. 'I can lift my hand. I can do that much. You supply the feeling.' And so woodenly, mechanically, I thrust my hand into the one stretched out to me. And as I did, an incredible thing took place. The current started in my shoulder, raced down my arm, sprang into our joined hands. And then this healing warmth seemed to flood my whole being, bringing tears to my eyes. 'I forgive you, brother! I cried. 'With all my heart!

Corrie Ten Boom found God in the midst of her deep disillusionment. Despite the darkness, she discovered a deeper understanding of His love. It freed her to become a capable, ethical servant leader for the rest of her life.

Unchecked, doubt and disillusionment often progress into the psychological state called depression– which is the topic of our next letter. Many leaders have struggled with it. We will address it.

"Now we see but a poor reflection as in a mirror; then we shall see face to face. Now I know in part; then I shall know fully, even as I am fully known. And now these three remain: faith, hope and love. But the greatest of these is love."-- 1 Corinthians 13:12–13

In solidarity,

Tom

LETTERS TO RISING LEADERS

Week 21 - Depression

THE PIT

A quick lightning strike of thunderclap sorrow
Blunt struck her to the ground as if by thief
Then stole her meager claim on tomorrow
Then shoved her in a dungeon pit of grief

She couldn't rise– the shoveled dirt rose higher
She couldn't move– the weight took all her breath
Inside the trap, dreams were rendered liars
And joy and hope and love were rendered death

Til her small, weak, heavy heart remembered
God's gift of never-ending, grace-touched love
Up rose two hands in desperate surrender
Down came two hands to grip hers from above

Back on the surface, still close is the pit
But God guides her way as she walks past it

Rising Leader,

You are humanity's hope. This is why your leadership preparation is
of utmost importance. Just look around. Ineffective, misguided,
short-sighted, selfish, compulsive and tyrannical leaders have
wreaked havoc on our world long enough. At this moment of peril,
we need capable, *ethical* leaders. This is why I write to you each week.
In these letters I seek to make some small contribution to your
growth as a servant leader.

Since this is my twenty-first letter to you, you now know what I
believe– that the best path to ethical fortitude is a deep and sustaining
relationship with God. Over the past twenty weeks I have explored
with you many aspects of that relationship, and its impact on ethical
formation.

Today, I wish to explore the psychological state called depression. At some point, all of us will experience it. This is because we all encounter loss, which brings grief. Depression is the fourth stage of grieving (denial, anger, bargaining, depression, acceptance).

For some, depression can rise up without an obvious prompt. There are even those for whom the torment of depression persists throughout life. How does one cope? And how does a leader experiencing depression continue to lead, with clarity and ethical fortitude? It's an important question for all leaders, whose decisions impact so many.

Abraham Lincoln fought depression his entire life. One man who knew him well said, "his melancholy dripped from him as he walked." Lincoln himself once spoke of "that intensity of thought, which will sometimes wear the sweetest idea thread-bare and turn it to the bitterness of death". Born into poverty in a log cabin in Kentucky and raised on the frontier, he became a lawyer and entered politics, experiencing both wins and losses until a fateful sequence of events elevated him to the presidency. Despite his ever-present melancholy, this greatest of American presidents led our nation through our darkest hour. How did he do it? What can we learn?

By 1860, Lincoln was on the precipice of the presidency. It was a time of rising tension and conflict in the United States, centered on the question of slavery. Two years previously, In his failed bid for a Senate seat, Lincoln had shined on the national stage– losing in a close contest to Stephen Douglas. The Lincoln-Douglas debates that preceded the election are to this day considered some of history's finest. In these debates, Lincoln clarified his own moral convictions and sharpened his arguments against slavery. Two years later, on February 27, 1860 Lincoln spoke in front of 1,500 people at Cooper Union's Great Hall in New York.

Before the speech, Lincoln was reported to be wearing a "woe-begone look". But as he took the stage, his haggard composure fell away. The passion of his convictions straightened his spine and captivated the crowd. As he spoke his final words– "Let us have faith that right makes might, and in that faith, let us, to the end, dare to do our duty as we understand it"-- the crowd went wild. The New York Tribune reported the next day that "No man ever before made such an impression on his first appeal to a New York audience." After the speech, a friend who escorted him to his hotel described Lincoln as follows: "No man in all New York appeared that night more simple, more unassuming, more modest, more unpretentious, more conscious of his own defects." He called him a "sad and lonely man."

Melancholy persecuted Lincoln for the rest of his life– through all the trials of his presidency and the terrible events of the Civil War. We have all seen the photographs of Lincoln as president, his face etched with crevices, his eyes sad and care-worn. And yet by all accounts, Lincoln was one of our greatest presidents. He ignited the conscience of the nation. He was a clear-eyed realist; he stared down truth and made difficult decisions that, at times, cost many precious lives. In the end, he saved the union. When it became clear the war would soon be won by the North, he worked to prepare all its citizens for the healing that would need to follow. In his second inaugural address, just 41 days before his assassination, he bestowed upon the nation the healing wisdom it needed most. Words now etched in history were first forged in his depression-tested journey of faith:

> "Each looked for an easier triumph, and a result less fundamental and astounding. Both read the same Bible, and pray to the same God; and each invokes His aid against the other… With malice toward none, with charity for all, with firmness in the right as God gives us to see the right, let us strive on to finish the work we are in– to bind up the nation's wounds, to care for him who shall have borne the battle and for his widow and his orphan– to do all which may achieve and cherish a just and lasting peace among ourselves and with all nations."

How did Lincoln lead despite his continuous struggle with depression? He prayed his way through it. When friends told him they feared for his assassination, his response was: "God's will be done. I am in His hands." He routinely read the Bible. God was his constant companion as he struggled with his tortured soul and sought pathways through the dark valleys of his life. In searing communion with God, Lincoln's moral clarity, humility and courage emerged.

Good leader, your bouts with depression may be brief and rare. Or depression may become a persistent cross, to be borne over the greater part of your life. I don't know why God allows bad things to happen to good people. All I know is that God is with us in the midst of our deepest, darkest moments. God the Father didn't rescue Jesus on the cross; He redeemed Him. And so it sometimes is with us. Even when no miracle comes to save us, He is with us. Sometimes all we may hear is silence– but God's silence can be trusted. He loves us with an infinite passion, and if we keep hold of His hand He will help us to transcend our deepest pain. Hand in hand with Him we will be led back to the land of the living; once there He will help us return to His work as best we understand it. There we will serve Him such as we can, for as long as we can, despite our many frailties and imperfections.

There are times when depression may even slide into despair. Next week's letter is about that.

"Answer me quickly, O Lord! My spirit fails! Hide not your face from me, lest I be like those who go down to the pit. Let me hear in the morning of your steadfast love, for in you I trust. Make me know the way I should go, for to you I lift up my soul."-- Psalm 143: 7-8

Your friend in hope and faith,

Tom

Week 22 -- Despair

PRODIGAL'S REUNION

The younger son demanded half estate
Then fled to distant country to debauch
To teach himself new levels of self-hate
To death-dance in the dark on bottom notch

The father, old, half-blind, nursed a habit
Of straining one good eye to scan the hill
Late came the day, as destiny would have it,
Through blur he caught a glimpse of figure still

In desperate hope he shuffled 'cross the clearing
The figure on the hill began to run
"Dear God in Heaven! If you're in my hearing
Please deign to name that running man my son!"

With joy exquisite, two frail hands of care
Embraced, forgave, and loved away despair

Rising Leader,

The cloak of loneliness that hung over Rich Mullins' heart for most
of his life was stitched early. Born to a meek Quaker mother and a
hard-driving farmer father, he grew up a disappointment. While
watching a "Cowboy and Indian" movie with his sister as a
four-year-old, he saw an "Indian" shot dead and burst out crying.
Attentive in church as a youngster, taking teachings seriously, he
soon became deeply attached to Jesus. His dad, a tough-leathered
Indiana farmer, tried in vain to stiffen his son's back and teach him
the ways of the farm. But Mullins was as soft as his father was hard.
He broke every implement he touched, including the tractor. A passion for music was sparked early by the attention of his great-grand-
mother, who taught him how to play hymns on the piano and sing
four-part harmony. His father once said ruefully, "I've got two sons,
two daughters and a musician."

Mullins carried his music and loneliness with him into the world—starting a band in college, and then becoming a church music director. After taking a group of church teens to a Christian music festival in Kentucky, he saw the power of music to connect with young people and decided to pursue it full-time. In 1981, Christian recording artist Amy Grant learned about Mullins and recorded his song *Sing Your Praise to the Lord*. It opened the gate that led him to become one of the best known Christian recording artists of all time. Two songs, *Awesome God* and *Sometimes by Step*, are to this day considered cornerstones in the cathedral of contemporary Christian music. Three of his albums are in the top 50 of all time (#3, #7 and #31).

In 1982, when his girlfriend-turned-fiancée decided she could not marry a professional musician, he said goodbye to the only woman he would ever love. He headed out on tour, traveling the country, singing to large crowds. In between gigs, he did missionary work in Asia and at a Navajo reservation, where he taught Jesus and music to children. Later, after his death in an automobile accident at 41 years old, these former students would speak with great love about their lost friend and spiritual leader. His success brought him riches, but he gave most of it away— choosing to live on the annual income of the average American worker, which was $24,000 at that time.

Despite his deep faith and through-and-through goodness, Rich Mullins wrestled with demons. He fought addiction to alcohol; at many low points in his life, he tried to drink away his despair. When his college friend's father (who had become a father figure to him) suddenly died of a heart attack, Mullins was inconsolable. So too when his fiancée left him. So too later, when his own father died. At these crisis moments, the bottle became Mullins' only friend. He performed more than a few concerts sick, hungover, and ransacked with self-loathing.

Despair is a crisis of faith. Surely God has deserted us. Hopelessness overwhelms; we feel naked, raw and empty. Utterly alone, our soul cries out into the vast silence with no expectation of reply. Our mind is wracked to exhaustion as we try in vain to rationalize our plight. Until finally we surrender the mind to the heart, and the heart to

God. Only then might a first flicker of light chance to pierce our darkness.

Somehow, time and again, Mullins found God in the midst of despair. His very vulnerability connected him with his audiences. His connection to Jesus was unshakeable; he knew his Savior saw him, loved him and walked beside him amidst his brokenness. It was enough.

In concerts, it was his habit to play a couple of songs and then stop to talk to his audience. In just such an interlude, he once said this:

> "God notices you. The fact is he can't take his eyes off of you. However badly you think of yourself, God is crazy about you. God is in love with you. Some of us even fear that some-day we'll do something so bad that he won't notice us any-more. Well, let me tell you, God loves you completely... And in the love of God there are no degrees, there is only love."

Later, he said:

> "I grew up hearing everyone telling me 'God loves you'. I would say big deal— God loves everybody. That don't make me special! That just proves that God ain't got no taste. And I don't think He does. Thank God! Because he takes the junk of our lives and makes the most beautiful art."

And he was not afraid to challenges his audiences:

> "Christianity is not about building an absolutely secure little niche in the world where you can live with your perfect little wife and your perfect little children in your beautiful little house where you have no gays or minority groups anywhere near you. Christianity is about learning to love like Jesus loved and Jesus loved the poor and Jesus loved the broken."

Rich Mullins' authenticity, humility and radical commitment to the poverty of Jesus flowed directly from the dark shadows of his soul.

Go online; listen to a couple of his songs. They drip with honesty. Anyone who has known despair will find solace in them. For example, check out the first two verses from his song, *Help Me Jesus*:

Well sometimes my life just don't make sense at all
When the mountains look so big
And my faith just seems so small

So hold me Jesus 'cause I'm shaking like a leaf
You have been my King of glory
Won't You be my Prince of Peace?

Mullins was a leader of great courage and consequence. His gifts of word and song blew like fresh winds through the stale air of institutional Christianity. Fearless in faith, he stood up to church hierarchy— challenging church leaders to embrace Jesus' radical call to serve the poor. He lived his Christian faith in service, focused on the fringes of the world. Through his music, he offered up his frailty and brokenness as a free-will gift of love. His Christianity was the big-tent kind. In search of a church to call his own, he checked out multiple denominations– Quaker, Lutheran, evangelical and Catholic– until he finally decided it didn't matter all that much, as long as he chose one: "...it's not about being Protestant or Catholic. It's about being faithful to Jesus."

Rich Mullins lived out the Gospel as best he could all the days of his life. By sharing his true self with the world through his gift of music, many thousands of broken souls came closer to Christ. "Never forget that Jesus died for you," he once said. "Never take lightly what it cost Him. And never assume that if it cost Him His very life, it won't also cost you yours."

For the past four weeks, we have explored the dark night of the soul in the shadows of doubt, disillusionment, depression and despair. Now, for the next four weeks, we will search out the beauty and joy that can be found by living true to our authentic selves.
"For the enemy has persecuted my soul; he has crushed my life to the ground; he has made me dwell in dark places, like those who have long been dead... I stretch

out my hands to You; my soul longs for You, as a parched land... Answer me quickly, O Lord, my spirit fails; do not hide Your face from me."-- Psalms 3-7

In fellowship and joy,

Tom

Song of the Month

SEE JOY, BE JOY

They knew it pretty early, something's wrong with Brett
Doc gave them Brett's prognosis, in words of kind regret
They brought back home their baby, a baby ever be
And Brett's young parents cried and said, "Why him? Why us? Why me?"

But tears dried by the morning, and in their place a smile
Their lives lay clear before them, in prayer they'd reconciled
Their lives would be in service to their stricken, precious boy
On that day they promised-- they'd do it all with joy

REFRAIN:

———-

What do you do with dreams that never happen?
What final letting go is required?
How can you make better out of bitter--
While sweeping up the hopes that have expired?

Go hold your hands and smile and count your blessings
Go trust in the abundant love of God
Each day's a gift when you begin with giving
Go choose to live with joy and love and awe

———-

In church as Brett grew older, he'd fidget and he'd yell
His Dad would lead him to the back to calm him for a spell
Brett's every-Sunday presence preached a different homily
In his complete dependence, a blessed sanctity

His Mom and Dad are seniors now, so Brett is in a home
It takes two helpers always, he can never be alone
Three times a week they visit their gift from God above
Whose quiet, steady, gentle stare is always filled with love

SECOND QUARTER: WHO AM I?

Joyful, joyful, we adore Thee
God of glory, Lord of love
Hearts unfold like flow'rs before Thee,
Op'ning to the sun above.

REFRAIN

Melt the clouds of sin and sadness
Drive the dark of doubt away
Giver of immortal gladness
Fill us with the light of day

Search "Tom Mohr– See Joy, Be Joy"
To find this song on YouTube, Spotify and all music platforms

LETTERS TO RISING LEADERS

Week 23 -- Behind the Mask

UNMASK

What Mardi Gras, Halloween life you lead!
Veiled behind intricate, desperate mask
Vanity's folly would be to succeed
In your selfward, illusion-conjuring task

For hidden beneath your fashioned facade
Is a shabby old soul, called to the dance
Called to sing beautiful music to God
Called to His splendorous, graced second chance

So fly to the true, O desperate soul!
Unfasten the bindings; loosen control
Turn your face to God, to be reshaped whole
Then dance to God's song like a stippled foal!

Do you seek to serve, leader, in God's employ?
Unmask into freedom. Unmask into joy!

Rising Leader,

No man stands alone. No woman is an island. We all exist in relationship– in space (neighbor to neighbor) and in time (from present generation to future generations). Our world is in crisis; the path towards
healing can only be traversed if capable, ethical leaders will rise up
and lead us towards goodness.

Perhaps you are such a leader. If so, it is on you to step forward, envision the fix, assemble your resources and begin to repair our most
precious human systems (planet ecosystem, diplomacy, democracy,
charity and worship). But this itself pre-requires soul work. This is
why I write to you each week, good leader. I wish to support you on
your journey towards goodness.

If you are good, you will do good. To be good, you must cultivate your relationship with God. This is the path to goodness. In daily communion with God, He will teach you how to remove the mask of your false self. He will help you discover the real you– your true self. Your true self is the person God created you to be– perfect in all your imperfections. You have gifts and gaps. You have loving tendencies– a big heart, a desire to serve. You have sinful tendencies– compulsions, biases, fears, things about which you are ignorant. You haven't fully healed from past hurts. You're a work in progress. But you try, day by day, to draw closer to God, to receive His love, to expose your soul to His inspection, to receive His grace, and to work on the things on which you need to work. When you do this, you are living out your true self.

The monk and mystic Thomas Merton describes a God-companioned journey towards the true self in this prayer:

> "My Lord God, I have no idea where I am going. I do not see the road ahead of me. I cannot know for certain where it will end. Nor do I really know myself, and the fact that I think I am following Your will does not mean that I am actually doing so.
>
> But I believe that the desire to please You does in fact please You. And I hope that I have that desire in all that I am doing. I hope that I will never do anything apart from that desire.
>
> And I know that if I do this, You will lead me by the right road– though I may know nothing about it. Therefore, I will trust You always, though I may seem to be lost and in the shadow of death. I will not fear, for You are ever with me and will never leave me to face my perils alone. Amen."

At many times in my life, I have lived out my "false" self. My false self is the mask I create to disguise my selfish motives– my desire to self-aggrandize, or to hoard, or to be better than– or to hide from view my hurts and regrets. When living out my false self, I attend to camouflage. I create an exterior illusion that enables me to do my selfish work or nurse my self-centered preoccupations undetected. When I live out my false self, I'm successful if I've kept myself beyond God's reach. I don't want His light, His love, His truth, His grace. I'm the pirate captain of my own tattered soul.

We all project to the world a public persona: our job, our educational background, the neighborhood we live in, our relationship status, the things we put on our Facebook and LinkedIn pages, the things we say when someone asks, "so what do you do?". There's nothing wrong with this, as far as it goes– as long as we recognize how transitory it all is; how utterly it pales in comparison to the eternal.

Behind that public persona sits our soul. It is here we must decide: will we commit ourselves to the God-centered daily work to nudge our public persona and our true self back into alignment? Or will we choose to fortify our false self more and more every day, so that we can run further and further away from God's love, truth and grace; so that we can bow down ever lower in idolatry to the god of our own ego?

For leaders– most especially for leaders at the pinnacle of power– this is a decision of profound worldly consequence. If we live out our true self, we find liberation. We are imperfectly authentic, imperfectly good. And we work on it with God every day. If, on the other hand, we cling to our false self, we begin a slow but steady slide away from God. Left unchecked, the slide accelerates. God gave us free will, to accept Him or reject Him. If our daily fortification of the false self continues through life, if the walls of self-delusion rise high enough, we will ultimately succeed: we will have banished God.

Only poison fruit grows from the tangled vines of the false self. We have all witnessed leaders, desperate to protect their power, avoiding the tough political choices to save our planet. We have seen leaders shrink from the moment with democracy under direct assault, for fear of the base. We all have seen how one power-crazed leader can destabilize the entire world.

The leader who has fallen into the trap of self-idolatry is a danger.

That's why the ethical state of our next generation of leaders is so vital. It is why I call out to you each week, rising leader, to take up the daily discipline of piety– to invite God into your soul every day– to welcome His love, truth, grace and joy. It is so that you can return to your true self; so that you can grow into a leader of goodness. The world needs you, servant leader. Only you and those like you.

Next week, we will explore what happens when finally we figure out how to move beyond ourselves.

"I will give you a new heart and put a new spirit in you; I will remove from you your heart of stone and give you a heart of flesh." —Ezekiel 36:26

Blessings to true you!

Tom

Week 24 -- Beyond Myself

TURN OVER GENTLE

Turn over gentle now, gentle that loam
Clay covers my soul; it traps me alone
Underneath it, I've nursed fears on my own
So pull up my sin, Lord; help me atone

Meager my fruits are; You know how I've strayed
In mulch of my poverty, plant me Your way
Set me in straight, well-rooted I pray
To sun-guide me upward— to grow day by day

Then transplant me humble into the need
Remind me the cross, where Jesus did bleed
Help me cast gentle now, gentle your seed
For only by You might each plant succeed

As rainfall and sunshine fall soft from above,
May furrow by furrow I seed with Your love

Rising Leader,

Please allow me to share today's message via an extended metaphor.

As I've emphasized these past few weeks, to lead with goodness, you
must become your true self. But to become your true self requires
that you welcome God into the castle of your soul. Yes, our souls are
castles, made up of three wings. The biggest wing is called Memories.
In this wing we find four rooms: Cherished Experiences, Hurts,
Regrets and Lessons Learned. The castle's second wing is one big
room: Fears. On the far side of the castle of the soul, there's another
one-room wing called Hopes and Dreams.

Once upon a time, a woman owned just such a castle. For many years
she had tended to it on her own. She had dug wide moats; built high

walls; watched daily from the guard tower with vigilant mistrust. But she was lonely. So one day, after much indecision, she decided to place at the gate a welcome mat for God. And so it was, on that very same day, a knock echoed across the courtyard. Lowering the gate, she saw that indeed it was God, standing at the edge of her soul.

She welcomed Him in, her smile timid as she beckoned. Her honored guest smiled back as He stepped inside. Together they crossed the courtyard and walked into the castle foyer. After taking His coat, she gave Him a short tour– showing off just her two most favored rooms (Cherished Experiences and Hopes and Dreams). God was friendly; she was talkative. It had been a long time since she had shared a soul walk with anyone. They both enjoyed their short visit, but soon it was over, and He was gone.

Weeks went by before God knocked a second time, this time asking if He could spend the night. Flustered, she blushed and deflected– it seemed such an unusual request. But in the end she said, "why of course!" and ran around to set Him up in the Hopes and Dreams room, well provisioned with prayer requests.

What a special guest He was. He asked thoughtful questions, and listened to her answers with attentive care. There was so much to talk about. At her request, He stayed on a few extra days, until one morning He asked if they might go on a tour of the entire castle. She hesitated. She thought, "isn't that a bit invasive?" Secrets were hidden in some of those rooms.

But in the end, she decided He was so kind and gracious, so caring, that perhaps she was ready to let Him in. In a march of momentary courage, she led Him into the room of Fears. "Oh, this room is quite a mess," she said. "Let's move on." Indeed, it was one big, messy room– filled with clutter and cobwebs. But God didn't join her as she edged towards the door. She watched in confusion as He took up a broom leaning against the wall. He began to sweep up the clutter, moving it all to the center of the room– where he proceeded to dump the pile into a trash can. He then began to swat cobwebs down from the ceiling. As He finished the task, He smiled at her. It seemed to her He was aglow with warmth and light.

As they came out of that room, she faltered; courage deserted her. But God walked past, strolling companionably towards the door of the room of Hurts. "Shall we go inside?" He asked. She stood frozen. But finally, hesitantly, she pulled out a key from her pocket and opened up the room. As He went inside, His movements slowed. He inspected the room with quiet care. Shattered shards lay all over the floor. He stooped down, picking up pieces of broken pottery. He began to arrange them on a table. Then He found some glue in His pocket and, piece by piece, began to put the broken vessels back together. Soon, many were back on their shelves, repaired, crack lines showing. All looked imperfectly beautiful. "These are your forgiveness vases," God said.

And then God took her hand. "It's time to enter into the room of Regrets," he said. At the door to this room, she hesitated again– and so God paused too. He looked at her with wrinkled, tender eyes. "Do you know how much I love you?" He asked. She looked up, tears flowing. Unable to speak, she nodded. "Then take my hand, my child. I am with you always." Into the room they went. It was dark and cold, filled with shadowy silhouettes. She stiffened. "There is no other way. You must face each shadow, my child," God whispered. "You are ready now. Name it, acknowledge your part in it, then ask Me to shine My light upon it and you. Only then will these dark shadows of regret disappear." And so she did– shadow by shadow, repentance by repentance, grace by grace. By the time she was done, the room was filled with light. She beamed. Boxes lined shelves, each named.

"Now let us take up these boxes. We need to move them to the room of Lessons Learned," God said. And so they did, box by box. Once the job was done, God brushed the dirt off His hands. He was about to leave when he noticed a box that had been there before they had brought in the new ones. He looked inside it, and a look of concern came over His face. "This box hasn't been packed properly. Things are in it that shouldn't be, and other things are missing. We need to take it back to the room of Hurts, so that it can be repackaged properly." This took some time; in fact, the task proved to be both difficult and painful for her. But eventually they were able to return the box, repackaged, to the room of Lessons Learned. With that, God smiled, turned and headed down the main hall, past the foyer, into the courtyard and towards the castle gate.

"But wait," she said. "Can't you stay longer?" He turned, quiet for a moment. "Of course I can," God replied. "But then you must allow me to rent from you. And if I rent, I must rent more than a room– I must rent the entire castle." It took a moment, but then she nodded.

Time passed; she settled into this wonderful arrangement. God and she visited the rooms of her castle every day, sweeping and arranging, shining light to banish new shadows and repacking and moving boxes into their proper places. But then one day, God came to her. He said, "Thank you for your hospitality, but I can no longer be your tenant." He began to gather His bags to leave. "But what do you mean?" she cried. "I need You! You must stay with me always!" God looked upon her with the most tender look of love. "My child, there is only one way that I will be able to remain inside this castle of your soul. The time for tenancy is over. For me to stay, you must sell me your castle. I will make you the tenant; I will be the owner and land-lord."

And this is how God came to own the castle of her soul.

On the day she handed over the title to the castle of her soul to God, she expected it would be an ending of some kind. But it wasn't the end. Nor was it the beginning of the end. Rather, it proved to be just the end of the beginning. Since that day, God has remodeled; He's expanded the size of the room called Hopes and Dreams. They still get together each day in that room, but the windows are larger— making it easier to look out into the world. In these daily get-togethers, God often points out the window, speaking of the world's hunger and need.

Just today, He encouraged her to go beyond the gate; to explore new pathways of the world– to find other crumbling castles, occupied by other lonely souls– and then to knock. Just this morning, He explained it to her this way: "My child, do you love me?" he asked. She replied, "My God, you know that I love you." With that He took her by the hand, walked with her through the castle and into the courtyard, lowered the gate and pointed out into the world. "Then feed my sheep."

Note: I first heard the "rooms of our soul" metaphor, and the companion notion that we are called to invite God to take ownership of the rooms of our soul, in a retreat led by Catholic priest Father Brendan McGuire. A servant leader of the highest order, Father Brendan is a gifted shepherd and heartfelt storyteller.

Next week, let's behold the beauty together.

"He said to him the third time, 'Simon, son of John, do you love Me?' Peter was hurt because He said to him the third time, 'Do you love Me?' And he said to Him, 'Lord, You know all things; You know that I love You.' Jesus said to him, 'Tend My sheep.'"-- John 21:17

In soulful joy,

Tom

LETTERS TO RISING LEADERS

Week 25 -- Behold the Beauty

I JUST LEFT

I just left. She was on her bed-on-wheels
Surgery beckons; they've come to roll her in
Hope, fright, powerlessness, plea-- that's how it feels
But it's love that fills my heart from deep within

In prep, we talked about our many blessings
The gratitude that animates our hearts
Then she took my hand and just began caressing
Until nurse came and asked me to depart

I love her. Three words so filled with beauty
Thank you, God, for all our treasured time
What this day will yield I can't yet see
But I trust Your holy, goodness-filled design

Never take for granted the beauty around you
Behold it. Cherish it. Let it astound you

Rising Leader,

Behold the beauty. Do you see it?

As leaders, our worldviews shape our decisions. Once our world-views widen to acknowledge the beauty all around us— in people, in nature and in ourselves— we are changed. We widen our circles of care. We find hope. We discover a gentleness of spirit. We become ready to celebrate beauty with others, which advances the good.

Can you see beauty in the people around you? There is beauty in a stranger's smile as she holds the door open, inviting us to walk through. Beauty is in hospitality with good friends. In our husband's or wife's hug in the wake of forgiveness. It envelops our last goodbye to our dying Dad. We can see it in the side-by-side stroll with our adult son as he describes his fiancee with wonder and love. It's in the homeless man's ministry to a drunk on the sidewalk. On a stroll through a Farmer's Market in springtime, we see it. In the crowds in Central Park on a sunny summer Saturday, we see it. Beauty is all around us.

Can you see it in nature? I remember when I first set eyes on the Grand Canyon from the south rim. I was hush-struck. There is beauty in the cut of a canoe as it glides through quiet water on a starry, starry night. It's in the outline of the majestic Himalayas, standing tall in the sky high above. It's in the crunch of snowy trails in Minnesota in February. It's in the cry of a coyote, the leap of a deer, the dart of a fox, the splash of a trout, the yodel of a loon.

Can you see it in yourself? There is beauty in the love we feel when we look upon our spouse and children. It's in the grace we experience when we finally make amends. It's in the peace we encounter in daily prayer. It's in the calm clarity that finally comes after a long struggle with confusion in our leadership roles. It's in the hope that comes when we realize that all of our time on this earth is just the beginning— an infinitely small fraction of eternal life in heaven with God. Beauty is in woundedness. Divine beauty shines at the crossroads of truth and goodness. We can see it even— especially— in the midst of human brokenness. The Irish poet John O'Donohue once said:

> "The beauty that emerges from woundedness is a beauty infused with feeling; a beauty different from the beauty of landscape and the cold perfect form. This is a beauty that has suffered its way through the ache of desolation until the words or music emerged to equal the hunger and desperation at its heart."

Have you ever witnessed broken beauty such as this? Have you ever been moved to step towards such human brokenness, perhaps to bring dignity, protection, help and healing? Good leader, broken beauty begs a love-response.

Beauty is in the sacred ordinary. Gerard Manley Hopkins captured it well in his poem *Pied Beauty*:

SECOND QUARTER: WHO AM I?

Glory be to God for dappled things–
For skies of couple-colour as a brindled cow;
For rose-moles all in stipple upon trout that swim;
Fresh-firecoal chestnut falls; finches' wings;
Landscape plotted and pieced– fold, fallow and plough;
And all trades, their gear and tackle and trim
All things counter, original, spare, strange;
Whatever is fickle, freckled (who knows how?)
With swift, slow; sweet, sour; adazzle, dim;
He fathers-forth whose beauty is past change:
Praise Him.

Beauty is in our God-carriers. These are the people in our lives, beautiful themselves, who point us to the beauty in plain sight. God-carriers are leaders; they are the ones who lead us to a better place. Beautiful inside and out, my wife Pageen is a God-carrier. From the moment of our first kiss to the moment I type these words, her love has nourished my hungry heart. Her Irish spark captivates me. And she teaches. Early on, she taught me to honor my faith by weekly church attendance. She taught me that my relationship with God would never sustain if I were to see it as just one of many spokes on my wheel of priorities. It had to be the central thing, the hub. Thirty-seven years on, she still teaches me every day. What a gift marital love is, especially as it yields the miracle of children. Mary Catherine and Jack have been God-carriers for Pageen and me from the moment of their births, to their first steps, all the way into their creative adult lives.

My Dad was a God-carrier. He gifted his integrity and love to me until the day he died. He gave me the beauty of his laughter, his love of family and his servant's heart. He taught me to love nature; to camp, to walk in the woods, to learn the names of the trees and the birds.

My Aunt Helen, still with us at ninety years young, is a God-carrier. She loved and prayed me through every struggle of my life. She remains to this day my closest spiritual advisor. There are others: the priest who once challenged me to join the board of a troubled

121

inner-city charity. The African American business leader who took me aside on a retreat and said, "It's good you talk the talk. When you step out of here, will you walk the walk?" My siblings are God-carriers, each in their own way. And then there are my closest friends, who hold me accountable each week to live out the best version of myself.

These are just a few of the God-carriers who have blessed my life. Who are yours? Seek them out. They will help you to see, through new eyes, the beauty within and around you. At our best, each of us is both teacher and student; leader and follower; a God-carrier and a God-receiver. Archbishop Desmond Tutu liked to quote an old African saying: "A person is a person through other persons." Beauty exists in our relationship to other people and things. When we behold the beauty, we become more interconnected-- more vulnerable-- more undefended-- more alive. To see beauty is to hope. With hope, we sense joy. With joy we sense possibility, which draws us into the world to become servant leaders. And so we become keepers of the beauty– God-carriers for others.

We are all participants in the miraculous music of life, with God interwoven. It's God who has placed us in His grand orchestra; it's He who has given us our instrument and who calls us to play our notes. When we follow God's baton, our contributions weave together with those of others to create a symphony of beauty that echoes through our souls. Behold the beauty.

I hope when you look in the mirror this week you will see your own interior beauty smiling back at you! Next week, we'll explore how to become the beauty.

"May the God of hope fill you with all joy and peace as you trust in him, so that you may overflow with hope by the power of the Holy Spirit."-- Romans 15:13

Beauty's blessings to you,

Tom

Week 26 -- Become the Beauty

DIVINE BEAUTY

Maples dewed and firelit welcome Fall's day
Canyon grand enacts its vast color-play
Arm-cradle warms by breath of sleeping child
A crosswalk-calm hand takes frail with smile

A pastor fields fraught midnight calls from flock
Someone takes pause for homeless man to talk
Soft prayer with prisoner who strives to endure
Salvation Army makes lodge for the poor

Concession speech humble, warm, gracious
Greta Thunberg; The United Nations
Nobel Peace Prize, Catholic Charities
Supply-chains for food for all refugees

Beauty gives, beauty heals and beauty protects
Will you become beauty, to step forward next?

Rising Leader,

We have all witnessed the dark power of leadership ugliness: its victims, its trail of tears, its devastation. We have seen how one world leader can single-handedly sabotage a nation's sovereignty and freedom, terrorize the innocent and vandalize the sculpture of geopolitical balance. We have seen the waffling of weak leaders in the face of the five-alarm fire of climate change. We have witnessed instances of leadership ugliness everywhere— in churches, in businesses, in communities. This is why, good leader, you are called to the dance. You must become the beauty the world needs.

Lived beauty is the antidote to all the world's hate, violence, ignorance and neglect. Are you such a leader? It is not an easy path. To discover your God-given interior beauty, you must accept the path of hardship. It's painful to audit your soul and confront your hurts and regrets. It takes courage to surrender, repent and seek God's grace. But if you commit to the work, your capacity to change the world for the good will be great.

The poet Robert Frost described it this way in his poem *The Gift Outright*:

> Something we were withholding made us weak
> Until we found out that it was ourselves
> We were withholding from our land of living,
> And forthwith found salvation in surrender.
> Such as we were we gave ourselves outright

The surrender to which Frost refers is surrender to God. From the scientists who tackle climate change to the practitioners of diplomacy to the defenders of democracy to pastors in our houses of worship, to all the people in key support roles throughout the world— we need leaders who walk daily with God. Piety points us to decency; decency leads us to civility; civility to charity; charity to democracy; democracy to diplomacy; diplomacy to sustainability. These are the seven disciplines of leadership goodness. Leaders who follow this upward path (from piety on up) radiate beauty. Their beauty draws others in. By this path, a leader's mission becomes a people's movement. And so we change the world.

Who planted into your soul your original goodness? From whence came your gifts and (for that matter) your gaps? God. The God of all Creation gave us all of these, along with a purpose. To pursue that purpose through the use of our gifts is our sacred duty and privilege.

Jesus showed us the way. He radiated His beauty, and it changed the world. He descended into the margins to find and save the poor, the sick, the lost and the sinful. And he kept saving and saving, until his last breath on the cross. What love-touched beauty when, naked and pierced to a cross, He said, "Father forgive them; they know not what they do." What healing beauty– when He saved the prisoner hanging next to him, saying: "Amen, I say to you, today you will be with me in paradise." What protective beauty– when He asked His disciple John to care for His mother Mary ("Woman, behold your son. Son, behold your mother."). What self-emptying beauty– when, sacrifice accomplished, He whispered Himself into the arms of God: "Father, into thy hands I commend my spirit."

Become the beauty, good leader. God calls; our world hungers.

In January, February and March, my weekly letters to you took up the question, "Who is God?". In April, May and June, they took up the question, "Who am I?". Now it's time to turn to the third quarter of our year, dedicated to the question, "Where's the Need?". For July, I will send you five letters that reflect upon American democracy. Then in August, I will share with you some thoughts on geopolitics and sustainability. In September, we'll explore church and community.

"Your beauty should not come from outward adornment, such as elaborate hairstyles and the wearing of gold jewelry or fine clothes. Rather, it should be that of your inner self, the unfading beauty of a gentle and quiet spirit, which is of great worth in God's sight."— 1 Peter 3:3-4

In love, beauty and joy,

Tom

LETTERS TO RISING LEADERS

THIRD QUARTER:
Where's the Need?

Week 27 -- Sacred Democracy

THE FLICKERED TORCH OF LIBERTY

In the end, America's built on trust—
that servants serve, that votes are counted fair—
that once the hot campaign is rendered dust,
the loser will concede with graceful air.

But when by foul cry faith is undermined,
aggrieved side chases compensating acts—
to tilt the scales to fix the ugly lie
that issued out of manufactured facts.

Which pricks the anger of the other side,
then shatters that side's faith in future votes.
One cycle, two, her raised torch flickers, dies—
last puff: democracy goes up in smoke.

Awaken now in nation God-borne truth!
Fast save integrity of voting booth!

Rising Leader,

There are many ways to govern a society: monarchy, oligarchy, dictatorship. Just one is sacred. Yes— it's democracy. Democracy flows
from God. God granted us free will; He granted us equal worth. He
created our diversity. He knows our fallen state. He made us unique
and interdependent. All of these make "government of the people, by
the people and for the people" sacred: checked and balanced,
self-healing, rejuvenating.

That's why democracy is one of the seven steps on the ladder I call
the "disciplines of goodness":

July 4th is around the corner. It's a day to honor our past. We do so by working towards a better future. One thing is clear about the future: America needs to renew its democracy. This can only be achieved with a fresh approach to leadership-- from both sides of the aisle.

At this tenuous moment, with the post-WWII world order now shattered in Europe and democracy under attack at home, we Americans find ourselves called yet again into the struggle for freedom. We enter this fight weakened and divided. American democracy is broken; we must renew and strengthen it if we are to be a force for good in the world. This work falls to leaders of goodness like you to return us to our shared values. As President Kennedy said in his inaugural address:

> "In the long history of the world, only a few generations have been granted the role of defending freedom in its hour of maximum danger. I do not shrink from this responsibility– I welcome it. I do not believe that any of us would exchange places with any other people or any other generation. The energy, the faith, the devotion which we bring to this endeavor will light our country and all who serve it– and the glow from that fire can truly light the world. And so, my fellow Americans: ask not what your country can do for you– ask what you can do for your country."

We are a nation divided. It is for that very reason that we must work together to protect our core institutions and values. Upon democracy's pillars the fate of our nation rests. For America to again become that "shining city on the hill", as Ronald Reagan once said, we all must engage in some deep and honest reflection. We must name what's wrong. Only then might American democracy be renewed– strengthened– protected.

First and foremost, we are called to value our democracy. You might have heard the phrase, "America is not a democracy— it's a republic". It is dangerous language. It legitimizes actions that work against democracy. Indeed, we are a republic— and a republic is a democratic form of government. It is composed of elected representatives, and an elected presidency. Ours is not a direct democracy, for sure; ours is a representative democracy– as most democracies are.

Our constitutional, representative, republican democracy enables equal and free people (not despots) to select their leaders and laws. The constitution marks the guard rails. Power is loaned to those leaders who emerge victorious from free and fair elections. In between elections, the rule of law prevails. By this way, peace is maintained; the common welfare is ensured; stability and change are kept in balance.

American democracy is founded on five pillars, all sacred ideals:

- Individual liberty
- Equal vote
- Equal justice
- Equal opportunity
- Truth

All of these ideals are of God. And all are at risk. A glance at the nightly news tells the story. We're beset by differences — seemingly irreconcilable. Our biases and fears make us vulnerable to the siren calls of one media silo or another. Caught inside our echo chamber of choice, we demonize those on the outside. In our debates, we can't even agree on the facts.

One fact was especially difficult for millions of Americans to accept: that Joe Biden won the 2020 election. This is not a Democratic truth, nor a Republican truth– just the truth. And it was and is the duty of every American to acknowledge it. It was certainly the duty of every Christian, called by God to live in truth. Since then, fact-free election denialism has shown its ugly head in other elections. It is a sin. Sacred democracy is built on trust, which is built on truth.

Yes, we have allowed the pillars of American democracy to weaken. Now we must work to strengthen them. A healthy democracy exhibits simple, universal voter access and sound vote tallying processes. It is pluralistic (multiple parties). It is one in which competitors fight fair (within the rules). It exhibits a transparent government. It preserves civil liberties. It features a free press. Sad fact: on most of these criteria, we are slipping. In 2021, the United States fell to the 26th spot on the Democracy Index (list of the most-to-least democratic nations)– below Costa Rica, Spain and South Korea. We are ranked a "flawed democracy". Another democracy review tool, Democracy Matrix, ranks the US a "deficient democracy".

Good leader, ponder what I'm about to say. It is of utmost importance:

> *The strength of American democracy*
> *is more important than our choice of party;*
> *is more important than our policy preferences--*
> *because democracy is a sacred gift from God.*

When we strengthen American democracy we are not advancing a policy. We are advancing our country. Whether liberal or conservative, Democrat or Republican, we all share a duty to protect and strengthen democracy. We are all called to live inside the guardrails set by our Constitution. At the most basic level, democracy requires losers to accept the loss and concede power. This is at the heart.

In our zeal for tribe, we too often lose sight of our most sacred ideals– the five pillars (individual liberty, equal vote, equal justice, equal opportunity and truth) that hold up our democracy. Too often, our demands for liberty have come at the expense of others'. Too often, we have seen our own vote as more important than others'. Too often, our demands for justice in one context have ignored injustice all around us in other contexts. We have approached "opportunity" as a win-lose proposition. We have marginalized the truth-tellers, bending truth to our views. We have become less respectful in debate, less tolerant, more judgmental, and now more violent.

This is not the America anyone wants — a house divided, weakened from within by cynicism and distrust. We yearn for a fresh, new and vital America — capable of embracing the future; of giving us life, liberty and the pursuit of happiness; of positive growth and change; of resuming its place as a beacon of hope for the world; of vigorous debate without damage to democracy itself. And so does God. Sacred democracy needs leaders who will protect it– especially at times of deep division. Leaders who might sing together, despite their differences: "America, America-- God shed His grace on thee."

Whether it be as servant citizens or as one called to elective office, we advance American democracy when we strengthen its pillars (the five sacred ideals). In the next four letters of this series, I will write about all five of these. It is especially important to advance them at times such as now, when we are in the thick of our sharpest debates. Never forget that democracy is of God. It sustains in the here and now because past generations fought to secure our generation's freedom– sometimes at great cost in blood and treasure. To be reminded of this, we need just look at Ukraine. Freedom is never free.

"When a land transgresses, it has many rulers, but with a man of understanding and knowledge, its stability will long continue."-- Proverbs 28:2

God bless America, and God bless you!

Tom

Song of the Month

AMERICA EVER NEW

America's changing
Spectacolor new
We're tugging and tearing
At opposing views

Cut left. Cut right. Quick, get in the fight!
Which side are you?

You bigot, you racist, you woke leftist mob
I'm right and you're wrong, get a life, get a job
Media silos channeling hate
There's only one way USA becomes great

Did you see what they did
Better tweet up a storm
We've got to escalate now!

Well, what do I do when what makes you free
Makes it not possible for me to be me
You might have your needs but I could care less
You are the reason we're in such a mess

Did you see what they did
Better tweet up a storm
We've got to escalate now!

And so we go, on down the road
Shouting and fighting, bickering, biting
And no one wants to be where we are
But we don't know how to stop, to reach past the trash talk

America's changing
Spectacolor new
And we can do better

THIRD QUARTER: WHERE'S THE NEED?

Both me and you

Today let's venture higher
Let's find civility
Let's join in hopeful choir
In ten-part harmony
Let's sing a brand new chorus
Let's sing our history
Let's sing what lies before us
Our new nation's liberty

America, bright shining star
God shed His grace on thee
And crown thy good with brotherhood
From sea to shining sea! Shining sea!

Search "Tom Mohr– America Ever New"
To find this song on YouTube, Spotify and all music platforms

Week 28 -- Democracy: Individual Liberty; Equal Vote

SAFEGUARD LIBERTY

What shame I felt when witnessed Jesus flag
waved high by mob that knocked down freedom's door
What pain to see my Savior on a rag
as if He'd led events deplored, abhorred

Is it not clear democracy best fulfills
God's twin benefactions bestowed at birth?
For with His gift of dangerous free will,
God gives us also love-kissed equal worth

This is why "of, by and for the people"
is the most sacred governmental form
The elected establish what's legal;
Their job to debate then enact our norms

The vote! The vote! Fair, pluralistic, free
This, only this, will safeguard liberty

Rising Leader,

> "Is life so dear, or peace so sweet, as to be purchased at the
> price of chains or slavery? Forbid it. Almighty God! I know
> not what course others will take; but as for me, give me lib-
> erty or give me death!"
> – Patrick Henry

> "Those who deny freedom for others deserve it not for
> themselves."
> – Abraham Lincoln

Once we recognize that God is in everything and everyone, we begin
to see and nurture our connectedness. We're all in it together, and
when we finally admit that, it becomes clear we must figure out our

137

way forward together. Through debate and compromise, we find our way forward. This is why God blesses democracy as the highest form of government. It's the only form that integrates His twin gifts of equal worth and free will. It's the only "let's-figure-it-out-together" form of governance on Earth. Which is why we are called to strengthen it, especially now.

America's changing. When I was born in 1955, America was 87% non-Hispanic white and 91% Christian. Today, America is 58% non-Hispanic White and 65% Christian. It seems to me our divisions stem in no small part from the tensions arising from our ever-growing diversity.

Like tectonic plates, "old" America and "new" America are in slow-motion collision. The old must slowly, inevitably give way to a rising new; the inexorable force of it makes that certain— but the jolts and tremors and earthquakes along the way are shaking our very foundations. That is why, as the ground shifts, our five core pillars of American democracy (individual liberty, equal vote, equal justice, equal opportunity and truth) must show both strength and resilience. Especially so for the first two of them.

246 years ago, the Declaration of Independence was passed by the Continental Congress. Its signatories pledged their lives, fortunes and sacred honors to the cause of liberty. Ever since, the notion of individual liberty has been central to our evolving American experiment. What is liberty, exactly? To have meaning, it must be attached to a "from". "From" is a relational word. From tyranny... from excessive government... from those who would compel or censor us. We Americans value our independence; it's woven into our constitution, history and stories. We are protective of our freedoms and distrustful of big government. We value free speech. We value our rights.

But as we declare our right to speak our truth, do we embrace the responsibility to hear the truth of others? As we declare our right to believe what we believe, do we respect the beliefs of others that run contrary to our own? As we pursue our right to economic opportunity and justice, do we demonstrate concern for the right of others to access equal opportunity and justice? God's call says we must.

Each of us has our vantage point. As a white, Anglo-Saxon American living in the suburbs west of Minneapolis, I enjoy, largely unimpeded, many fruits of handed-down liberty. But I have a friend– a fellow Christian who has served with me in prison ministry work– whose shoulders are not as unburdened as mine. My African American friend lives near Santa Monica, CA. He boasts an MBA, a rising-middle-class job and a nice car. And about once every three months, as he drives around his neighborhood, he gets pulled over by the police. His shoulders are (unlike mine) weighed down; his liberty hemmed in.

Individual liberty and equal vote are two God-given, sacred principles at the very core of our democracy. And both are at greatest risk at times of the greatest division. Of course, liberty cannot mean freedom to do whatever we want. Individual liberty does require boundaries— though never due to police bias, such as my friend has experienced. As the free swing of my fist meets the end of your nose, my right to liberty ends. Yours takes over. Time and again in our diverse nation, liberties sought by one group have come into conflict with liberties claimed by another. It seems to me that as important as individual liberty is, we must hold it humbly and carefully– recognizing the need to balance ours with others'. Ultimately, this balance can only be found within the workings of our democratic system. And within the workings of our hearts, with God by our sides.

As I have repeated throughout these *Rising Leader Series* letters, all people and things exist in relationship– with God interwoven. Yes, we are unique– but we are also interdependent. This is why equal access to the vote is so fundamental. Voting rights and individual liberty are two sides of the same coin. In our liberty, each individual exerts the freedom of thought and speech so essential to a healthy democracy. Each of us has the right to express our needs and views. Doing so enriches the contest of ideas at the center of the democratic process.

But that process must also be free and fair. As important as individual liberty is, we must also respect that every American is of equal worth— worthy of an equal vote. To seek to lessen the voting power of a competing group is to attack the foundation of our democracy.

Gerrymandering, voter suppression measures, and secretive vote-counting are wrong. Yet all of these happen. Where is our righteous, universal condemnation? Who will mobilize a bipartisan movement to push back on such fundamental threats? Perhaps it falls to you, good leader. So much does.

We make democracy healthy when we debate our competing ideas and claims in free and fair elections; when we cast our votes (via mail or in person) free from complicated steps; when losers concede and winners win as determined by transparent vote counts; when victors are sworn into office without disruption. As I said in my last letter to you:

> *The strength of American democracy*
> *is more important than our choice of party;*
> *is more important than our policy preferences--*
> *because democracy is a sacred gift from God.*

Our American citizenship comes with the duty to fight for everyone's liberty; everyone's equal vote. When these are threatened, we must all take notice and act. Do you see that this is our divine call? Protect the vote. To those who call themselves "Christian", yet seek to tilt the scales to give their side an edge, I say "God forbid". For to rig democracy is to slap the face of Jesus Himself.

Next week, we will explore the third of the five core American ideals: equal justice.

"So Peter opened his mouth and said: "Truly I understand that God shows no partiality..."-- Acts 10:34

Yours in liberty and equality,

Tom

Week 29 -- Democracy: Equal Justice

THE LAW, THE LOCK AND THE KEY

By vote we choose the ones who write our laws
By rule of law our nation keeps the peace
Peace officers enforce the same for all
For all so safety, freedom will increase

But sometimes written laws are ill-conceived
And sometimes perfect peace is not well kept
And sometimes officers are right perceived
As biased, heavy-handed, maladept

Which is why we citizens ever must
Seek ceaselessly to winnow out the true
To filter facts so as to co-construct
A union more secure, more fair, more glued

Brave is justice served free from fear or favor
When mixed with mercy, it's much better– braver

Rising Leader,

Rwanda, Turkmenistan, El Salvador and Cuba have something in
common. They all make the "top 5" list in their prison incarceration
rates. But none can beat us– the United States. We're #1. Think
about it. As you read this, over 2 million people are incarcerated in
our country– up 500% in the past 40 years. Over half are Black or
Hispanic.

What's wrong with this picture? One of the five pillars of American
democracy is equal justice. Yet in our laws, in policing, in sentencing,
in corrections practices and in rehabilitation practices– we have not
yet achieved it. It remains the work of leaders like you to do so. That
is how we form a more perfect union. Jesus countered hate with love
and sin with forgiveness. He had a way of continuously keeping love,

truth and grace in balance. Are we not called to do the same? This is how we do what Jesus would do.

Our laws define what is a crime; each crime has its punishment. But it's easy for laws to be written unjustly.

Powder cocaine (known as the "white" drug of choice) was once subject to much lighter penalties than crack cocaine (known as the "black" drug of choice). And so our prisons filled up with black and brown faces. Lives were ripped asunder. Though this specific inequity has been corrected, it underscores how important it is for laws to be written with care and fairness. When not, it tears at the fabric of our democratic system– making justice unjust.

Even when crime is justly defined in law, sentencing guidelines can be unjust.

Ever-longer prison sentences don't reduce the crime rate. All they do is destroy lives. Despite our elongated prison terms, America's crime rate is worse than 81 countries in the world. We need to remember that punishment is just the first step in redressing a wrong. The goal is repair. We need leaders of goodness who will craft just laws– with sentences designed not just to punish, but also to reform and heal– and ultimately to repair the world.

Once laws are on the books, they must be enforced.

Living as I do outside of Minneapolis, I have struggled with two conflicting narratives about policing. Both hold some truth. The world witnessed the abomination of George Floyd's death, face pushed to the street under the knee of a police officer. We were all stricken to the core. It triggered an eruption of righteous anger, both in the US and around the world– in no small part because across America, black and brown men die far too often at the hands of police.

But it is also true that police forces across the country are filled with dedicated, courageous public servants. Their jobs are difficult and dangerous. Many police officers have retired or quit; departments are understaffed. Some believe that many who remain, fearing a deadly incident, have begun to shy away from appropriate enforcement. Now let me be clear: we can't remain silent in the face of police brutality and racial profiling. Policing must be re-envisioned, reformed and continuously improved. However, it's also true that we can't ignore the reality of crime, nor how dangerous it is to fight it. There are now over 120 guns for every 100 people in the US. Since George Floyd's death, the rate of crime (especially violent crime) in Minneapolis and cities around the country has skyrocketed.

Enforcement is a difficult task, requiring ethical officers capable of exercising good judgment and great self-control. We need leaders of goodness to lead and staff our police forces— leaders who will get enforcement right, so that all people can enjoy peace, safety and equal (and just) protection.

Judges also have a difficult job.

A just sentence redresses the hurt incurred by the victim, while also pointing the perpetrator towards correction, reform and, ultimately, rehabilitation. It's on judges to weigh the law and its sentencing guidelines. Within those guidelines, they must weigh the facts of the case— and determine proper punishment. Yes, the debt to society must be paid. But it's equally important to repair the world. We can't just keep building prisons to lock away more humans. We need judges who will deliver justice both blind and equal, mixed (wherever possible) with pathways towards reformation and rehabilitation.

Part of the problem is how we see prisoners and their victims.

I once served inside a maximum security prison as a member of a prison ministry retreat team. Prior to that experience, I had categorized prisoners as "them"-- the "other"-- the "bad guys". And it's true that most prisoners are in prison because they have done bad (and in some cases horrific) things. But still— the chasm between "them" and "us" shrinks when you meet one-on-one in a direct, personal encounter. I came away changed from that retreat.

I learned... hurt people hurt people. Crime has a blast radius; it wounds the victim, perpetrator, families and friends. It tears at our interconnectedness. It destroys trust and engenders hate. All too often one crime begets the next– drawing entire communities into a descending cycle of violence. And all are human beings, sinners yearning to be loved. Behind the tallest walls, beyond our most manic defenses, every heart seeks God. Towards the end of my weekend prison ministry retreat, one prisoner said: "My soul was parched like a dying plant, shriveled on the ground. Now I'm watered. I'm filled up. I can feel my heart again."

Once we connect with the humanity of both victim and criminal, once we recognize both as brothers and sisters in the human family, the question of justice becomes less cold– less abstract. God never gives up on us. The Bible is filled with repentant sinners (Moses: murder; David: murder and adultery; Paul: hate crimes and false imprisonment). Once they saw their sin and truly repented, God forgave them– and then used them to advance His kingdom. When it comes to crime and punishment, might it be that we too are called to balance punishment with mercy?

Our justice system is punishment-centric, but perhaps not victim-centric. Many victims seek more than punishment. Many wish to confront– to better understand– and, often, to forgive. Regardless of the response, forgiveness can be a way to let go and move on. I once met a woman whose family had been torn apart by a home invasion, rape and murder. After the perpetrators were sentenced and imprisoned, she decided to participate in a restorative justice program– wherein she could confront the perpetrators of this horrific crime. She described it this way: "I needed to tell them that I don't hate them. I forgive them. Now, that does not mean I support letting them out of prison. But I cannot hate them. And by sitting down to talk I can set myself and them free in a way that no one else can."

It seems to me our encounters with victims and prisoners must be both clear-eyed and humble. Victims rightly expect the state to pursue justice. They also need and deserve both love and support. Crime exacts a terrible toll; proportional punishment is just. But we must never forget that the purpose of justice is, in the end, to heal– to restore the victim, to reform the perpetrator and to repair the world.

We all fall short of the glory of God– we're all a work in progress– and it's never too late for any human being to turn back towards goodness. Equal justice is delicate work, which is why its pursuit requires leaders of goodness like you.

Next week we'll take a look at equality of opportunity.

"Then he added, 'Now go and learn the meaning of this Scripture: 'I want you to show mercy, not offer sacrifices.' For I have come to call not those who think they are righteous, but those who know they are sinners.'"-- Matthew 9:13

In justice and peace,

Tom

LETTERS TO RISING LEADERS

Week 30 -- Democracy: Equal Opportunity

SHOULDERS OF HOPE

Great-granddad landed young on freedom's shore
From street to street, sold coal in the city
His son, my PopOps, sold stuff door-to-door
So his son could make it to university

That man, my father, chased down two degrees
First Wesleyan, then Harvard MBA
Went on to find the American dream
For which his forefathers worked, paid and prayed

Does any co-citizen deserve any less?
Chance first to learn, then to grow, then to dream?
Help others attack the blocks to success!
For by this path is your privilege redeemed.

Each of us stands on our forefathers' shoulders.
For whom will your shoulders be the upholder?

Rising Leader,

Equal opportunity is one of the five bedrock ideals in American
democracy, because opportunity bequeaths hope. Hope is of God; it
binds us together. Lack of opportunity snuffs out hope, which under-
cuts shared allegiance. Can we expect Americans who have lost all
faith in the future to remain faithful to our flag? Whenever any citizen loses hope, American democracy is weakened. To strengthen
democracy, we need leaders who will confront the corrosive patterns
that eat away at equal opportunity.

God gave us equal human worth; we all have equal access to God's
infinite love. But our human gifts vary. We vary in our innate personal attributes; we vary in our efforts to learn. As a result, talent will
vary, even with equal access. Talent begets a job, which begets

wealth. Every American deserves equal opportunity to test the boundaries of his or her God-given potential. When birth-endowed gifts are cultivated by equal opportunity, people can pursue their dreams as far as talent and ambition will take them.

The state of opportunity in America affects the state of our democracy. Democracy can end swiftly by direct attack– such as an insurrection, coup, or invasion by a foreign power (as Russia has attempted in Ukraine). Or its pillars can be weakened gradually by the acid rain of corrosive patterns. To protect and strengthen American democracy, we must confront both.

Corrosive patterns eat at equal opportunity; our country needs good leaders like you to stand up to these patterns and envision pathways towards renewal. Renewal is most needed in four domains:

- Access to quality education
- Business liberty
- Federal debt
- Sustainable growth

Access to a quality education matters.

My Harvard-educated father built a successful career, which afforded my siblings and me the best education money could buy. We lived in the right school districts, received lots of parental encouragement and were given the necessary financial support to go to top tier colleges. This opened the door to high-promise careers of our own, enabling us to do the same for our children.

Yes, I am a product of privilege. Such privileges are not available to most Americans. The cost of college is beyond reach for many. This is why college financial aid and student-friendly student loan programs are so important. Sadly, inequality crops up even earlier. Public schools aren't all equal. This is why America's investment in public education is so vital, as is private school innovation– especially in underserved communities.

For five years I served as a founding board member of Cristo Rey San Jose, a private Jesuit high school in Northern California whose 500-person student body is predominantly Latino. Most parents of Cristo Rey San Jose students did not go to college; many did not graduate from high school. Due to benefactor support and its unique one-day-a-week student job internship program with partnering businesses, Cristo Rey offers a top tier private education at a bargain-basement tuition cost.

Students entering Cristo Rey as freshmen are, on average, two grades behind in math. Through the hard work of the students (and their teachers), average math scores rise to a ninth-grade level within six months. Throughout the four years, teachers reinforce the goal: to get a college education. It is inspirational to see the light of opportunity turn on for the first time in a student's eyes. To sit in the stands at the annual graduation ceremony, to know that 95% of graduating students were accepted to college, to see their smiles and the joy of their parents, is a blessing to behold.

A mind is a terrible thing to waste. No matter the background, never doubt a child's potential. Time and again I've seen what a quality education can do to transform a life. Equal access to quality education is sacred; achieving it takes leadership.

Business liberty matters.

Small business creates two-thirds of all American jobs. Jobs are the wellspring of opportunity. Overregulation is a corrosive pattern. Imagine the owner of a small machine shop or restaurant, trying to remain compliant with the labyrinth of city, county, state and federal rules and regulations. It's an undue burden, forcing owners to work late into the night and on weekends– filling out all the forms, calculating all the taxes and fees and dealing with compliance issues. Regulatory overreach strangles business opportunity and steals jobs from regular Americans. As prosaic as it seems, to simplify regulatory requirements is to strengthen American democracy. This too is a leadership challenge.

The federal debt matters.

As of today, the US federal debt stands at over $30 trillion. This equates to $243,000 per taxpayer and rising– and it's unsustainable. Our debt will rob opportunity from our children and their children. They will ultimately shoulder the crippling burden of our excess. Deficit spending is a corrosive pattern that weakens our democracy. Good leader, America needs you to envision a way out– to find a way for us to live within our means, so as to preserve the American dream for your children and theirs.

Sustainable growth matters.

Capitalism has shrunk world hunger, elevated average life expectancy and improved standards of living around the world. But it has also decimated the Amazon, polluted the seas and skies and depleted the world's natural resources. Unchecked capitalism is a corrosive pattern. Good leader, we need you to envision new guardrails to build around American capitalism so as to make growth more sustainable, so that we protect opportunity for future generations.

Equal opportunity breeds hope. With hope we dream. Our dreams inspire us, unite us and draw us back to our flag. All Americans deserve a chance to live the American dream. By making opportunity more equal, we follow God's call and strengthen democracy.

Next week, I will write to you about truth-- and its role in democracy.

"So whatever you wish that others would do to you, do also to them, for this is the Law and the Prophets." – Matthew 7:12

May all your dreams come true,

Tom

Week 31 -- Democracy: Truth

IN DEFENSE OF JOURNALISTS

We've lost them by the thousands o'er the years
As broadcast news and papers shrink and die
Replaced by platforms amplifying fears
With strident voices spewing battle cries

Each day sets flight to fresh but unchecked "news"
Which stains the public trust as if by blight
Repeated, becomes treated as if true
A murder of crows blocking out the light

Against this swarm, far, far too few persist
In honoring their sacred public pact
Praise God the independent journalist
Who investigates then verifies the facts

Brave journalist: beat back the threats that lurk!
Democracy depends upon your work

Rising Leader,

God calls us to live in truth.

Truth is the fifth of the five sacred pillars that undergird American democracy. We can't sustain the other four (individual liberty, equal vote, equal justice and equal opportunity) without it. Its importance to democracy is profound in no small part because it checks the ambitions of the powerful. Truth informs: it settles elections; it holds all to account; it can disrupt the master narratives of elites; it challenges the biases we all keep in our heads; it opens our eyes and widens our circles of care. America needs leaders who will safeguard the truth.

Perhaps you will feel called to the public trust, good leader. If so, your constituents will expect nothing other than the truth from you.

We need leaders of goodness throughout our government who act from a strong ethical core.

But the reality is that God gave humans free will. Too often in real life, leaders fall prey to the calculus that a lie yields more power than the truth. Perhaps the truth would disrupt a governing party's narrative, or a political allegiance, or one's own political standing. Thus comes the lie.

Many in power believe that to control the master narrative is to perpetuate power. This is why dictatorship holds such hidden appeal to the corrupted leader. Dictators possess the means to punish truth and control what citizens hear. And it works, at least in the short term. We see this now, in Putin's Russia. It is on the rise as well in our own United States, as truth-bearers are attacked and punished by keepers of the lie. Awaken to the threat, good leader; make truth your shield.

Adolf Hitler wrote the dictator's playbook in his book, Mein Kampf. Here's an excerpt:

> "The function of propaganda is… not to make an objective study of the truth.. its task is to serve our own right, always and unflinchingly… The receptivity of the great masses is very limited, their intelligence is small… In consequence of these facts, all effective propaganda must be limited to a very few points and must harp on these in slogans until the last member of the public understands what you want him to understand by your slogan. As soon as you sacrifice this slogan and try to be many-sided, the effect will piddle away…"-- Adolf Hitler, Mein Kampf

Psychological research studies show that once a group comes to deeply believe in an untruth, almost no amount of evidence can overturn that conviction. That is why, if not checked, lying is such a corrosive pattern. In a democracy, a free press provides the means to counter attempts by elites to control the narrative with lies. Here are excerpts from the Journalist's Creed, written in 1914 and still taught to this day. It is grounded in Godly principles:

- I believe that... accuracy and fairness are fundamental to good journalism
- I believe that suppression of the news, for any consideration other than the welfare of society, is indefensible
- I believe that... a single standard of helpful truth... should prevail for all; that the supreme test of good journalism is the measure of its public service
- I believe that... journalism... is stoutly independent, unmoved by pride of opinion or greed of power, constructive, tolerant but never careless; self-controlled, patient, always respectful of its readers but always unafraid; is quickly indignant at injustice; is unswayed by the appeal of privilege or the clamor of the mob; seeks to give every man a chance and, as far as law and honest wage and recognition of human brotherhood can make it so, an equal chance; is profoundly patriotic while sincerely promoting international good will and cementing world-comradeship; is a journalism of humanity, of and for today's world

Robert McCormick, founder of the Chicago Tribune, once said, "The newspaper is an institution developed by modern civilization to present the news of the day... and to furnish that check on government which no constitution has ever been able to provide." But in the past twenty years since the rise of the internet, the business model of traditional print and broadcast media has broken down. There is no viable return to that lost world of powerhouse newspapers in every metro area and above-reproach news anchors from three evening news channels prioritizing and broadcasting the day's truth. It's a new world. Journalism must adapt, good leader, so that the truth may continue to shine.

How can truth emerge in a world awash in social media and online news? To be clear, social media can be (and often is) a force for good. Everyone has a smartphone, so everything can be documented. Video clips of the murder of George Floyd, the killings in Bucha, politicians saying impolitic things– these are the raw materials of news in today's world. We are always on, and the world is watching.

Bellingcat is an example of a new journalistic entity using the data from social media and other digital sources to expose corruption and political violence. Bellingcat did just this to track down, confirm and name every member of the assassination team sent to poison Alexei Navalny, the opposition leader who ran against Vladimir Putin for the Russian presidency. The Bellingcat team proved the trail led right back to Putin. Using similar methods, it also unmasked the Russian and separatist perpetrators of the downing of Malaysia Airlines Flight 17 over Ukraine in 2014. Digitally-sophisticated journalistic teams such as Bellingcat are a force for good.

But on the leading media platforms, it's also true that hate rages and misinformation is rampant. It's on each platform to make up its own rules for policing misinformation and moderating debate. The problem is with incentives. Since ad revenue is highest when rhetoric is sharp and debate runs hot, the public's need for truth and the platform's need for profit don't align. As such, manufactured conflicts and conspiracy theories– such as QAnon, the stolen 2020 election narrative, or the "vast right wing conspiracy" narrative— often overwhelm journalist-validated news. Some rising media outlets don't even pretend to seek objective truth. Advancement of their own tribal narratives is their sole mission. Stoking conflict, they've learned, is the better path to profit or power.

For the average citizen, this daily flash flood of information and misinformation overwhelms. Each media source gushes its daily stream; collectively they assault us with rumor, fiction, silliness, debauchery, fact, real news, half-baked analysis and opinion. Confronted by this daily slag pile of noise, how can the average citizen sift out rare diamonds of truth?

Many of us do it by narrowing our focus areas down to our most familiar outlets. But this creates its own problem. When we tune in only to the sources most custom-fit to our own pre-shaped narratives, we lose sight of the bigger picture and lose touch with competing narratives. This makes it easier for us to to amplify grievances; to name and blame enemies. Our hand-picked "news", information and opinion pay homage just to our existing biases. It may feel safer and more self-gratifying, but to live solely inside these echo chambers is not a good thing. If we are to grow as individuals and as a nation, we all must suffer the discomforts of a wider truth.

Democracy needs journalism, much as a boat needs a keel. Journalism no longer controls what the world sees (as it did in the pre-Internet era)– but nonetheless it still plays a vital role in advancing truth. We need journalists to verify news accuracy, prioritize what matters most, dig deeper when needed, and provide context– always independently, always with rigorous accuracy, without fear or favor.

Is this your call, rising leader? If so, may Jesus guide you. Jesus brings the truth you must know, wrapped in love. He insists upon justice, but mixes it with mercy. His goal is not to condemn, but rather to reform, renew and save. As you work to advance the truth, good leader, you would do well to do the same. In the end, truth births awareness, accountability, repentance, forgiveness, reform and renewal. Truth is of God.

Next week, my letter to you will take up the subject of diplomacy-- another step on the ladder I call the "disciplines of goodness".

"Stand firm then, with the belt of truth buckled around your waist, with the breastplate of righteousness in place"— Ephesians 6:14

Yours truly,

Tom

LETTERS TO RISING LEADERS

Week 32 -- Diplomacy

THE DIPLOMAT'S PRAYER

Dear God, our flag and theirs are waving hate
Outrage has peaked; two calls to arms begin
Do You not grieve as we mass to storm the gate,
both of us follied certain that we'll win?

They cry: "No use our tools of war but war!"
"Our cause is true; the hour has come for might."
"Quit using words as means to settle scores!"
"Diplomat, quit the stage so we can fight!"

Despite the fevered pitch, Lord, still I chance
To lean on You– to learn Your peaceful path
I yet invite my counterpart to dance—
In tiptoed waltz towards way to curb the wrath

God, help us trick the odds; come sheathe our swords
Then lead us, act by act, towards trust restored

Rising Leader,

You will recall the ladder of virtues I've referred to in past letters as
the "disciplines of goodness":

The second highest rung on the ladder is diplomacy. Diplomacy is the art of resolving conflicts without violence, while serving the legitimate interests of each side. Diplomats seek first to understand, and then be understood. They seek win / win solutions. They seek to turn the table around, so all parties find themselves on the same side– looking together at the problem to be solved.

My father was a diplomat. After my mother died when I was eight years old, Dad remarried. By then I was thirteen. Suddenly, my younger brother and sister and I were welcoming three new siblings into our home. I now had a sister nine days older than me; I had two brothers two months apart; two of my sisters were named Debbie.

As the oldest child, I had become accustomed to certain privileges. I actually can't remember what they were, but at the time they seemed important. Like putting the final ornament on the Christmas tree– that kind of thing. Well, after the wedding, in our first week as a new Brady Bunch family, Dad declared that all "oldest sibling" privileges would now be handed over to my slightly older sister. It infuriated me. It was just the first in a series of diplomatic acts taken by my father. He knew he needed to signal we were "one family" by actions large and small. From the day of our two-family-into-one unification, to the day I headed off to college, life at home was chaotic. Conflicts abounded. Every time it seemed as if things would spin completely out of control, Dad would intervene with the perfect mix of listening, challenging, incentivizing and sanctioning. He had a way of pulling us out of our small-circle spats, and helping us to see a bigger picture. He taught respect. He taught the importance of family. My Dad was a great diplomat. The fruits of his work grace my life and those of my siblings to this day. We are close– as close as any loving family can be.

Diplomacy is also vital on the global stage. Time and again, it has saved the world from disaster. On October 14, 1962, Major Richard Hayser, flying a high-altitude mission over western Cuba, photographed an SS-4 ballistic missile battery being assembled on the ground. With Cuba just 90 miles from Florida, a functioning missile battery would give the Soviets the capability to execute a lightning-fast nuclear strike on the US. President Kennedy was notified on October 16, and for the next thirteen days the world skirted the edge of the nuclear abyss.

Within the close-knit team that advised the President, some advocated an immediate attack on the installation. President Kennedy, chastened by the failed Bay of Pigs invasion and conscious that such an attack risked immediate nuclear war with the Soviet Union, demurred. On October 22 he announced to a shocked nation the presence of the installation and ordered a naval blockade around Cuba. Privately, he sought contact with the Soviet leadership. Letters were exchanged. Diplomats shuttled messages back and forth. Tensions peaked when, on October 27, a U-2 plane was shot down over Cuba, killing the pilot. Speaking of that day, US Secretary of Defense Robert McNamara later said, "I thought it was the last Saturday I would ever see".

Ironically, it was on that same day that a breakthrough was achieved. Attorney General Robert Kennedy traveled in secret to the Soviet embassy, and met there with Ambassador Anatoly Dobrynin. Sitting privately with the Ambassador, Kennedy delivered a final offer. The US would take down its own missile battery in Turkey, if the Soviets would dismantle theirs in Cuba. But there would be no deal unless the Soviets agreed the dismantling of the Cuban battery would be made public, while the dismantling of the Turkey installation would be kept secret. Khruschev was as sobered by the risk of nuclear war and mutual annihilation as was Kennedy. He too was looking for a way out. The Soviets agreed. Missiles were taken out of Cuba and Turkey, and the world lived on.

The Cuban Missile Crisis was the closest of close calls. It was only through a series of carefully orchestrated acts of diplomacy– by Kennedy, Khruschev, UN Secretary General U Thant, the ambassadors on both sides and trusted diplomats working for these men– that all-out nuclear war was averted.

As humans, we live with the threat of nuclear weapons, with tyrants and despots, with leaders who come to power by demonizing other peoples and nations, with governments constantly scheming to seize geopolitical advantage. In our communities, we live with tribal divisions and too much bigotry and hate. In our churches, we live with imperfect leaders and power struggles and doctrinal conflicts. In our families, we live with tensions, competition and hurtful experiences. It is within this broken world of ours that the diplomat works, seeking tirelessly to advance the good– to de-escalate conflict, to repair schisms, to nudge all parties towards respect and— dare we say it— love.

In the end, people all around the world are much the same. We all seek survival, security, freedom, opportunity and (most of all) love. As I've said from the beginning of this series, everyone and everything is connected, with love interwoven. When we begin to see God in all things and in each other, we become capable of expanding our circles of care. We begin to identify with the legitimate needs and interests of others, while still respecting our own. This capacity to understand, to care, to balance our own needs with those of others– these are the essential competencies of diplomacy.

Whether it be to preserve global peace, to advance racial harmony in our communities, to bridge differences in our churches, or to stitch together a family– the art of diplomacy is one we are all invited to take up. The world needs diplomats: capable and ethical. The Jewish Talmud teaches, "We don't see things as they are, but rather as we are." Our natural orientation is to live inside a small circle, seeing things from just our own narrow perspective. It takes diplomats to stretch our circles wider.

So God bless you and all diplomats. May you find a way where there is no way; may you bring us peace on Earth and goodwill to all humankind.

Next week's letter will be the first of three on the topic of planet sustainability.

"God shall judge between the nations, and shall decide for many peoples; and they shall beat their swords into plowshares, and spears into pruning hooks; nation

shall not lift up sword against nation; neither shall they learn war anymore."
-- Isaiah 2:4

Peace be with you,

Tom

Song of the Month

RISE UP

Have you ever seen New Delhi, have you been to Kathmandu?
Those Himalayan mountains climbing up into the blue
Summer lakes in Minnesota, Singapore alive at night
What a world of beauty and delight

The coral off of Queensland features fish of many hues
The Serengeti lions roam, gazelles and leopards too
San Francisco in September is such a pretty sight
What a world of beauty and delight

But temperatures keep rising by degrees
Progress has our planet on its knees
Before we choke on too much smoke
And flee the rising seas
Rise up, rise up humanity

The Colorado river fills the taps of the Southwest
The Amazon rainforest makes oxygen the best
The north pole and the south pole need to stay big sheets of white
To keep our world of beauty and delight

Have you seen the Southern Cross, have you seen the Northern
Lights?
Have you tasted sweet clean water on a cool summer night?
The God of all Creation speaks a silent mighty plea
Rise up, rise up humanity

In our hands we hold our children's children's children's children's
fate
Across the mists of time they plead to act before too late
To unleash the wealth of nations, marshall all our human might
To save this world of beauty and delight

Have you seen the Southern Cross, have you seen the Northern

THIRD QUARTER: WHERE'S THE NEED?

Lights?
Have you tasted sweet clean water on a cool summer night?
The God of all Creation speaks a silent mighty plea
Beloved
Beloved
Look around
And see
Rise up, rise up humanity

Search "Tom Mohr– Rise Up"
To find this song on YouTube, Spotify and all music platforms

Week 33 -- Environmental Sustainability

EVENING PRAYERS FOR EARTH AND US

Lord, remnant forest canopy please keep
In Greenland, save the final sheets of ice
African elephants: seed and breed them free
Queensland's coral: reverse hot sacrifice

Turn Southwest's tap, to stream at widow's wish
Settle the seas that smash too high on shore
Sprinkle oceans with new swarm-schools of fish
Spark stratagems to soil the skies no more

Lord, help us save beauty of broken Earth
And so honor our children's children's cries
For You, O God, gave us a purposed birth;
Your call resounds in silent plea to rise

Lord, shake us out of apathetic gaze
May we rise strong in action-woven praise

Rising Leader,

Astronauts speak with awe of their first view of our planet from outer space. From afar, there it hovers: our solitary Earth, hanging in space at just the right distance from the sun, with just the right atmosphere to sustain life. What a spinning miracle it is. From the perspective of space, how insignificant our fevered squabbles must seem; how appalling our carelessness.

If only we could wear astronaut eyes. Who would not be struck to the heart by Earth's beauty and fragility? Our connectedness is so obvious from space. And then we look closer... closer... closer. We see machines at work, tree-stripping the Amazon. We see billions of us, carbon-soiling the skies– fish-scouring the seas– coal-gashing our mountains. Day by day we slash and tear at the web of our God-given, love-woven connectedness. And we call it progress.

My wife and I recycle. I've ordered an electric car. But are we careful in our use of plastics? Have we done enough work to minimize energy use in our home? No– not yet. We need to do more. I suspect this might be true with you as well. In every community, most every household can make a bigger difference to advance the sustainability of our planet. But it's also true that the actions of individual households will just scratch the surface. The most impactful actions humanity must take need to unfold on a massive scale. To decommission fossil fuels, we must spin up vast new global energy sources (such as nuclear fusion, hydrogen, solar and wind). To clear the air, we must construct global-scale networks of carbon-sucking machines. To promote sustainability, we must reshape the laws that regulate all national economies in the world. And then to support the millions of people dislocated by these actions, we will need to mobilize transitional retraining and support. It will require a level of sustained sacrifice and collaboration never before seen in the history of humanity.

Everything and everyone is connected– with love interwoven. God endowed us with our Earth, brimming with beauty and bounty. He gave us dominion over it. But for centuries we have abused God's gift. And now He pleads with His people to awaken and rise up. "Come to the aid of your Mother Earth– no matter the cost, nor how long it takes," God calls. He speaks to leaders just like you. Scientist, banker, investor, entrepreneur, pastor, legislator, diplomat: the fate of your children's children's children is in your hands. The moment is now. Will you rise?

After the attack on Pearl Harbor, Franklin Delano Roosevelt said:

> "Yesterday, December 7th, 1941—a date which will live in infamy—the United States of America was suddenly and deliberately attacked by naval and air forces of the Empire of Japan… The attack yesterday on the Hawaiian Islands has caused severe damage to American naval and military forces. I regret to tell you that very many American lives have been lost… As Commander in Chief of the Army and Navy, I have directed that all measures be taken for our defense… No

matter how long it may take us to overcome this premeditated invasion, the American people in their righteous might will win through to absolute victory."

Here's what he did not say:

"Yesterday, December 7th, 1941—a date which will live in infamy—the United States of America was suddenly and deliberately attacked by naval and air forces of the Empire of Japan… As Commander in Chief I have ordered our Army and Navy to respond with small and partial measures. I am not at all confident we will win— in fact, we probably won't. In the end, perhaps it will be best to kick the can down the road and let the next generation deal with it. We'll all be gone before it really matters."

Truth hurts. If we don't cap the rise in temperatures and the corresponding rise in oceanic acidity within 25 years, most coral reefs in the seas will die, becoming vast gray underwater cemeteries. Drought grips the West as we dither; we are frozen in indecision as 120-degree days pan-fry New Delhi and eighty-degree days bake Alaska. Glaciers melt. Seas rise towards levels that threaten every coastal city and town in the US and around the world. Want to see an elephant? Do it now. They're critically endangered.

Climate change. Loss of biodiversity. Pollution. Land and sea degradation. Our planet needs you, good leader, to rise up— now. There's still time to act, but there's no time to waste. Great work must be done at epic scale and significant cost, which requires great global will. All of us need to do so much more, more quickly. And so, good leader. As you stand on the podium before your country and the world, the ghost of FDR has a question for you. Which speech will you give?

Ask not what your planet can do for you, but what you can do for your planet. Next week, let's explore how our economy impacts sustainability.

"So God created humankind in his image, in the image of God he created them;

male and female he created them. God blessed them, and God said to them, 'Be fruitful and multiply, and fill the earth and subdue it; and have dominion over the fish of the sea and over the birds of the air and over every living thing that moves upon the earth.'"-- Genesis 1: 27-28

Yours in sustaining faith,

Tom

Week 34 -- Economic Sustainability

THE WHOLE WORLD IN MY CUP

Gold-touched was August's morn as I rose.
Bullfrog croaks joined cricket crepitations
with finch-cheep, robin-cuck, chickadee cry
as trout-splash bothered mallard's machinations.

Observed from white-gloss Adirondack chair
Hand-hot coffee; shimmer-diamond lake
A place to ponder planetary care
and contemplate the work that it will take

How muster global will to build constraint?
What path to, step by step, repair the Earth?
That some future child of God might acquaint,
like me, with gold-touched summer morn's rebirth?

I sat tempted for a moment to give up
Until looked down, saw whole world in my cup

Rising Leader,

We protect God's creation by building a sustainable economy.

Marty Odlin grew up on Maine's coast, close to fishermen and their boats. When he was young, fish hauls were bountiful– but over the years boat yields steadily declined. By the time he was ready to buy his own boat, he realized the math wouldn't work. The sea had lost its capacity to offer a fisherman enough fish to make a living. Warming seas, rising acidity and overfishing had precipitated a crash in fishing stocks, even over the course of his short life. But Odlin knew how critical fish are to the food supply chain. And so he decided to do something about it.

Odlin recognized the source of the problem was the rise of carbon

dioxide in the atmosphere. It was causing the warming and acidification of the seas. Scientists agree that to heal the planet, billions of
tons of carbon dioxide will need to be removed from the air and the
ocean. To do this, carbon capture and sequestration technology
needs to be deployed on a massive scale. And so he built a company,
Running Tide, to do just that.

Running Tide is working to deploy thousands of solar-powered
buoys in oceans all across the globe. These buoys are constructed to
sustain micro-forests of seaweed; each carries a few pounds of limestone. Seaweed feasts on carbon; limestone feasts on acid. Odlin
believes that if enough of these buoys were deployed around the
globe, they would substantially reduce carbon in the atmosphere and
acidity in the seas. HIs company is also building oyster farms, which
act to filter and cleanse ocean water. Billionaire investors have
invested in his company. The future looks bright.

Our blue planet is one big interwoven life form, with God in all of it
and us. Everything and everyone is connected; we are composed of
bits of the stars. I like to say we live in a state of interbeing with God
and each other. But God has given us free will; our actions have consequences. Certainly they have impacted the intricate web of inter-
connections that make up Mother Earth. Day by day, our actions
create the civilization in which our children's children's children will
live. If we truly love our own descendants, then, we will demonstrate
our love by working to create a better, healthier world. We can only
do this by creating an economy that sustains life on Earth.

What is an economy? It is a human construct. It is composed of
rights, requirements, incentives and constraints. In America, we possess the right to private property. We enjoy the right to invest and
create new businesses. We are required to pay employees a minimum
wage, to follow labor laws, to report our income and to pay taxes.
Government subsidies create incentives; tariffs, taxes and fees create
disincentives. Regulations create constraints. Within these rights,
requirements, incentives and constraints, citizens are free to work, to
innovate, to start companies and to pursue their dreams.

A sustainable economy is one designed to steadily improve the intricate system called our planet. In systems, inflows cause stocks to rise; outflows cause stocks to fall. God has gifted our solitary galactic home with a set of precious, life-giving stocks: clean air, clean water, forests, fish and wildlife. These are the building blocks of human existence. It is madness to deplete them.

But for the past three hundred years, that is just what we have done. We have built an ever-more-extractive global economy, permitting a steady net outflow from our most critical stocks. In pursuit of growth and rising standards of living, we have paved the way for individuals and companies to take without replenishment– to deforest, to overfish, to pollute land and sea and sky, to kill off species. Today's blaring sirens– rising temperatures, diminished air quality, reduced fishing yields, acidification of the oceans, shrinking reservoirs, species extinction and more– are our planet's feedback loops, alerting us to our peril.

Now that the pace of planetary degradation has put the future of human life on Mother Earth in doubt, we face a key question. Is our economy (with its rights, requirements, incentives and constraints) built to advance sustainability? Are the economies of other nations? The answer, of course, is "No". And yet all economies must become sustainable economies– and soon. Which means, good friend, we need you. Humanity needs its most capable and ethical leaders to stand in the gap– to lead us away from our extract-and-run economy, into a truly sustainable one– constructed with new rights, new requirements, new incentives and new constraints. This is, more than anything, a political problem. We need courageous, capable, ethical political leaders to rise up and show us the way. Are you one?

If you build such an economy, you will inspire leaders like Marty Odlin. He has accomplished much without a US carbon tax, or other adjustments to our economy's rights, requirements, incentives and constraints. Imagine what could happen if America and other nations were to actually implement sustainable economic regulations such as these.

Planetary degradation is the road to death. Along that road, every act of degradation is another violence. Sustainability is the road to God and life; every planet-healing act is an act of love. It's really that simple. In the end, we humans must ask ourselves: which road? Will we choose death and violence, or life and love?

Today is the seventh day, good leader! The time is now. We need you. Next week's letter will take up the topic of social sustainability.

"And God said, 'Behold, I have given you every plant yielding seed that is on the face of all the earth, and every tree with seed in its fruit. You shall have them for food. And to every beast of the earth and to every bird of the heavens and to everything that creeps on the earth, everything that has the breath of life, I have given every green plant for food.' And it was so. And God saw everything that he had made, and behold, it was very good. And there was evening and there was morning, the sixth day."-- Genesis 1:29-31

Sustainably yours,

Tom

Week 35 -- Social Sustainability

MAY OFFERINGS SAVE

Forgive– I know not what starving children feel
Nor mother, water vanishing from well
Nor father, as crops fail– sheep die– death steals
Nor tribe nor nation caught up in such hell

Nor fully understand the hard transition
That workers by the millions must traverse
as, in a blink, built skills are decommissioned
And the need to start anew nags like curse

I can't conceive, because I'm born to privilege
Its grease has ever smoothed an uphill ride
Yes or no: will I return advantage?
Heaven awaits upon me to decide.

Yes, my God, Yes: please transform what you gave
Into gifts returned, with love, so to save

Rising Leader,

Last week, I wrote that humanity's survival depends on creating a sustainable global economy. We need you, good leader, to construct your nation's economy in such a way that it promotes the healing of our planet-- God's creation and gift. To make the necessary difference, we must do so for every nation, every economy on Earth. But as important as this is, it is not enough. As we execute this sustainable-economy shift, God challenges us to figure out how to bring everyone along.

Rich countries such as ours have historically been the biggest polluters. Today, as standards of living rise around the globe, planet degradation is metastasizing. Just consider the planetary impact of China's and India's modernization, each with 1.4 billion citizens on the rise. Affluence is growing, and affluence pollutes.

And yet here's the sad irony: affluence creates poverty. Whole communities are made poor by the decline of fisheries, rising seas and rising temperatures. And so when an impoverished mother needs to keep her family warm, she chops the last tree down because it is her only available source of fuel. When an impoverished father needs to buy grain to feed the family, he kills the elephant because an elephant tusk fetches good money. Affluence, poverty and planetary degradation go hand in hand in hand.

God willing, soon– over the next decade– the entire world will adopt sustainable economic structures. As sustainability begins to be built into every economy on Earth, the lives of millions will be disrupted. What will happen to the coal miners and oilfield roustabouts and gas station owners and their families when we finally transition away from fossil fuels? Whole sectors of our economy will be taken out of service; new ones will arise. Peoples' lives will be upended. And so, good leader, it is not enough to create economic sustainability. We must build the infrastructure and support systems to create social sustainability.

This is a human challenge. Every human being is of equal worth and dignity. This is God's worldview; it should be ours. First-world nations are called to partner with leaders of goodness within third-world and second-world nations, so as to co-create sustainable emerging economies. First-world nations have polluted the most; we must also offer remediation and support to those third-world nations that will bear the brunt of rising seas and rising temperatures.

Leaders throughout the world will need to mobilize retraining programs for workers, on a massive scale. What job options does an out-of-work coal miner have? This is not just the miner's problem; it's a problem we all own. That's what it means to expand our circles of care. If impacted families are to traverse the space between "from" and "to", they will need both our financial and our emotional support.

None of this is easy. Where will the money come from? How will we ever achieve the political will to spend so much to help disadvantaged countries sustainably develop? How does it square with our need to rein in the national debt? No, it won't be easy. That's why we need a new generation of capable, ethical leaders to rise. Good leader, perhaps you are the one called to this noble task. It's not a job for just anyone; it requires great moral clarity. For if we are to heal our planet and achieve a sustainable world, we will need leaders who can bring the whole human family together. Each of us must help each other along the way.

In this work, we serve the marginalized and dislocated. So it has always been: God's continuous call is to widen our circles of care; to reach out to those most in need. What would Jesus do? He would go to the need. His path was the descending path. He sought out the poorest of the poor: the widow; the orphan; the sick; the marginalized. He taught his disciples that to love the least is to love Him. Just so, He calls out to you now. Will you go?

Next week, my letter to you will explore leadership within the church.

"Then the King will say to those on his right, 'Come, you who are blessed by my Father; take your inheritance, the kingdom prepared for you since the creation of the world. For I was hungry and you gave me something to eat, I was thirsty and you gave me something to drink, I was a stranger and you invited me in, I needed clothes and you clothed me, I was sick and you looked after me, I was in prison and you came to visit me.' Then the righteous will answer him, 'Lord, when did we see you hungry and feed you, or thirsty and give you something to drink? When did we see you as a stranger and invite you in, or needing clothes and clothe you? When did we see you sick or in prison and go to visit you? The King will reply, 'I tell you the truth, whatever you did for one of the least of these brothers of mine, you did for me.'"-- Matthew 25: 31-40

May you raise the torch of your goodness high, good leader, so all can see the light of your love.

Tom

Song of the Month

PALMS TOGETHER

CHORUS:

———

Down, down, down we go
'Til our knees fall to the floor
Palms together, Hands held high
We give thanks to Christ our Lord

———

When two or more of you are gathered
Christ is there in your midst
Come with thanks to His table
Come share in His gift

CHORUS

Come to church you heavy-laden
Caught inside your self-made cage
Bring your cares to precious Jesus
Your Lord and Savior age to age

CHORUS

Life is short and time's a-wasting
Jesus needs our helping hands
He needs His church to build the kingdom
But first let's give Him thanks

CHORUS

We give thanks to Christ our Lord

Search for "Tom Mohr— Palms Together"
To find this song on YouTube, Spotify and all music platforms

Week 36 -- Church: Encounter

IRRITATING NEIGHBOR

An irritating neighbor called out "Welcome!"
As I ran out my brand new home one day
Handed me a pie-well-dressed, called key lime
I tight-smile grabbed it, then went on my way

She knocked again on Saturday, that Laurie
So in the morning sun we sipped some tea
She opened up and shared some of her story
But she got precious-little out of me

Next week, arms-on-fence, she offered greeting
As I was digging in the garden by the birch
I felt a shock-of-warmth come up so fleeting
That lingered-warm when said, "come to my church"

Surprise! I found such smiling people there...
But how explain the tears that welled in prayer?

Rising Leader,

Let me share with you a story.

Hearing a loud knock, a priest jumped out of his lounge chair and made his way to the door. Standing in front of him was a young woman, two ragged-looking kids in tow. "May I help you?" he asked. "Yes," the mother answered. "I'm down on my luck. I need money for groceries." The priest took a step back, closing the door just a smidge. "This isn't how it's done," he said. "Aren't you on welfare? Have you been to the soup kitchens? Maybe they can help you." Her tired eyes locked on his. She stood mute for a long time. Finally, she said:

"Are you going to lecture me or help me?"

The priest who answered the door that day was Father Arnold Weber. During the years our kids were growing up, he was our beloved pastor at Holy Name of Jesus Church in Medina, MN. From the pulpit, he often spoke of that day– how it changed him– how it turned upside down his entire notion of "church". In the fragile, fleeting space between that mother's call for help and his own response, Fr. Weber discovered the real church. From that day on he pastored from a fresh perspective– one that was more love- and service-centered.

The real church is not a building. It's not an organization, nor a business (though any individual church must deal with organizational and business issues). It's not just doctrine– not just a set of rules. It's not just a parish, nor even a denomination (such as Catholic or Lutheran or Pentecostal or Presbyterian). The real church is the body of Christ– continuously reaching out to church-goers and non-church-goers, the young and the old, Evangelical and Catholic, sinners and saints (we all tend to be one or the other on any given day), the confused and the alienated, the ashamed and the haughty, the caught-up, the just-getting-by and the utterly-disconnected– all in need of God; none beyond the reach of His love. The real church exists to bring people back to Him. To open our whole hearts to Him. To create an interconnected and joy-filled Christian community centered in Him . To lovingly serve in the world for Him. The real church appeals to that yearning in all of us for the divine, for authentic fellowship, for accountability, for purpose, for love. And the Holy Spirit lives within it.

In this time of change, Christianity needs leaders who will make our churches more real. This requires renewal in two domains:

- Its heart
- Its fringes

What is the heart of the Christian church?

Love. That's the heart of the church. Jesus' entire life was expressed in love. Father Arnold was such a good pastor because he lived,

178

spoke about and guided us towards God's love. As I have said many times in these *Rising Leader Series* letters, everything and everyone is connected– with God interwoven. God is love; he seeks for us to be love-immersed– to be with Him and in Him. And as much as He delights in our private prayers, He also calls us into community– to become members of a church. As Jesus said, "Where two are more are gathered in my name, there I am in the midst…" (Matthew 18: 19-20) Lay ministers, the clergy, you and me– we are all the church. Each of us, in our own way, is called to live and share the love of God.

Whenever we get too caught up in our hierarchy and dogma detail and rituals and purity tests, we begin to lose this essence. As we preach church doctrine, let us never forget that the heart of the church is love.

What is the mission of the church at its fringes?

At the fringes, the mission of the church is to serve and to welcome. This is the call of every Christian. An inward-facing, rigid, doctrine-obsessed church is of no help to God. He calls His church to step out and descend, as Jesus did, into the world– to find the lost, to heal the wounded, to support the widow and the orphan. "They Will Know We are Christians by our Love" is a beautiful song, and its title says it all.

The outward-reaching church, as it works on the fringes, is sure to encounter souls ready to receive a "come-join-me-at-church" invitation. There is sacred fragility in this moment; how we extend our invitation matters. If we lecture, her heart might close again. We might lose touch forever. But if we offer our invitation with a warm smile, she might take that first step. Once inside the church, if we sit together, if the message from the pulpit is welcoming, if brokenness and woundedness are acknowledged as part of our human condition, if she senses hospitality and love and support, then she might show up again the next Sunday– and the next. By such small steps a soul comes to know God.

Of course, our soul work is never done. Like free-range chickens, we humans tend to wander away from God's love. Suddenly we look up and realize we are in danger. The job of the church is to continuously reach out and welcome us back from wherever we have wandered. The real church reminds us of our original goodness. It alerts us to our disconnectedness. It helps us encounter God in prayer and in each other. It leads us towards repentance and God's grace. It helps us accept God's forgiveness (so we can forgive ourselves). It draws us deeper into church community. It guides each of us towards our own unique call. And it challenges us to go into the world and follow it with love.

It may seem that the tide of Christian followership– especially in first world nations– is fast receding, with Gen Z and millennials most caught in the rip curl. It is true: church attendance is in decline. But beyond the frenzy of modern life, behind the false masks of our caught-up egos, the soul's hunger remains. And God's table of plenty awaits, just inside the doors of His church. God calls out for leaders capable of opening the doors and meeting this hunger with the truth of His love and call. As with all of humanity's greatest problems, it comes down to a problem of leadership. Will you be the change our churches need?

Come, good Christian disciple. Your church needs you. Spark a fresh new movement of the faith: a movement grounded in compassion and guided by the Holy Spirit. A movement working at both the heart and the fringes of the church. Come lead with a smile; lead with authenticity and humility. A young woman stands before you: she struggles to feed her children, to find hope and to discover meaning in the midst of suffering. As she stands there, she poses one simple question to you, and to the entire Christian church– on behalf of billions like her all around the world who hover at the fringes of the faith: "Will you lecture me or will you help me?"

Next week, we will explore Christian discipleship. Our church needs disciples to lead it. Come to the table, you who are heavy laden, and find rest beside us. For together we are the body of Christ!

"And He said to him, 'You shall love your God with all your heart, and with all your soul, and with all your mind.' This is the great and foremost commandment. The second is like it, 'You shall love your neighbor as yourself.' Upon these two commandments hang the whole Law and the Prophets.'"—— Matthew 22: 37-40

Yours in body and Spirit,

Tom

Week 37 -- Church: Discipleship

AS SUN AND I ARISE

As sun and I arise, my Lord, I greet You
To share this bright new day in prayer before You
Shine light on sin, that I might seek grace from You
To ready my soul so that I might serve You

Prepare me, then, to be Your humble servant
Pray banish from my heart all selfish thoughts
Replace within a heart-fire ever fervent
That brings me to my knees before the cross

And if it be Your will that I should lead,
Pray keep my gaze fixed firm upon Your face
That in Your Church Your work through me succeed
Well sheltered in Your love-imbued embrace

Take all of mine, my Savior, make it Thine–
Small contributions to Your grand design

Rising Leader,

In the years before World War II, Dietrich Bonhoeffer was a rising star in the German Lutheran Church. Ordained at age 25, he took up pastoral duties at Old-Prussian United Church in Berlin. In his inspiring and theologically rigorous sermons, he spoke with conviction and authority. Soon word got around; he rose in prominence. But this was Germany in the thirties. As Hitler began his ascent– and as the teachings of the Gospel got in Hitler's way– Godly leaders became a threat. Indeed, Bonhoeffer was a threat— because he saw Nazism for what it was. At great risk, he became an outspoken opponent of Hitler and the evils of Nazism.

The institutional German Lutheran Church didn't do the same. It became infiltrated with Nazi sympathizers. A movement arose to purge church leadership of all who carried even a trace of Jewish blood. Soon came the call to banish the Old Testament– it was too Jewish. Preachers began to claim Jesus was not a Jew; that Jews were the perpetrators of Jesus' death; that the entire Jewish race was illegitimate and forever stained.

Bonhoeffer fought hard to wrench his church back from the demonic abyss– but the forces of evil were too strong. In the end, after all his efforts had failed, he came to the painful conclusion that the German Lutheran Church was irredeemable. It had fled the Holy Spirit; it had abandoned the Gospel.

And so he departed to form a new, Gospel-centered church. It was an act of great courage, since it was a direct rebuke to the Nazi regime. He called it The Confessing Church. He opened up a seminary so as to teach young men to become its pastors. Soon the Nazis got wind of it, discovered the seminary's location and shut it down. Bonhoeffer went underground. He continued to instruct and ordain new pastors for the fledgling church. The Confessing Church lived on, its services conducted secretly in German homes. As long as he could, Dietrich Bonhoeffer kept the flame of Christ alive in the midst of utter darkness, right under the eyes of the Gestapo. In the end, he paid for his discipleship with his life.

In his book, *The Cost of Discipleship*, Bonhoeffer describes discipleship by differentiating between cheap grace (which avoids it) and costly grace (which embraces it). Says Bonhoeffer:

> "Cheap grace is the grace we bestow on ourselves... the preaching of forgiveness without requiring repentance... grace without discipleship, grace without the cross, grace without Jesus Christ...
>
> Costly grace confronts us as a gracious call to follow Jesus. It is costly because it compels a man to submit to the yoke of Christ and follow him; it is grace because Jesus says: 'My yoke is easy and my burden is light.' ... It is costly because it costs a man his life, and it is grace because it gives a man the only true life."

We must acknowledge that across Christianity's history, the church has all too often lost its way-- invariably due to weak or misguided leaders.

Consider my Catholic Church. It has been a force for great good in the world-- from the individual faith formation of billions, to the survival of Western philosophy via scribes in monasteries, to great schools and universities and hospitals all around the globe. Across the ages, leaders of goodness have sought to serve Jesus by giving their lives in service of the Church.

But in its long history, there have been times that the Catholic Church has gravely erred. Corrupt Popes have impoverished the people to fund their own excess-- fruits of ungodly greed and lust for power. The Church initiated the Spanish Inquisition (300,000 died). The Crusades (5 million died). The Doctrine of Discovery (which gave Apostolic blessing to European colonizers to "invade, search out, capture and subjugate all Muslims, pagans and any other unbelievers... and to reduce their persons into perpetual slavery"). More recently, leaders turned a blind eye to the horrific scandal of priest abuse. No, my Catholic Church has not always been a force for good.

Protestantism arose in opposition to a wayward Catholic Church. Its leaders sought to build churches more aligned with Jesus and the Gospel; less hierarchical; less centralized; less money-centric. Protestants printed the Bible and preached in local languages, making Christ's message more accessible. Over the past 200 years, it was mainstream Protestant churches at the forefront of the abolition-of-slavery movement, the women's suffrage movement and the Civil Rights movement.

But Protestants were also the ones who tried many women for witchcraft, killing 40,000 of them. Most early Protestant Christian leaders, including Martin Luther, were deeply anti-Semitic; Protestant and Orthodox Christian vilification of Jews over the centuries contributed to the deaths of millions in the Holocaust and earlier pogroms. It was Protestant American settlers who coined the phrase, "the only good Indian is a dead Indian". For over 300 years, some large Protestant church denominations used the Bible to defend slavery in

America. Even to this day, there are certain Evangelical churches that have bound themselves to the extreme wing of one political party.

Remember: the church is both divine and human. And at times, pride or power lust or rigidity or small-circle thinking might tilt the ratio human. So we must be alert, good leader. For the church is us. Not just the pastors and inner circle administrators-- all of us. When our churches fail to teach Jesus' radical love, it is on us to rise and challenge. We also must encourage, and support. It's hard to lead the flock. It's a collective effort; God needs all of us to keep the church true to Jesus' love.

A friend of mine describes vigilant leadership this way: "Keep on top of things. Because things are either green and growing, or ripe and rotting." Sometimes what's needed is a nudge-- to do the more courageous thing. For instance, much is taught from the pulpit about personal morality. But in most churches, systemic morality receives barely a mention. It's too touchy. Racism, social justice, the defense of democracy, respect for differing beliefs, equality and respect for all regardless of sexual orientation, planet sustainability-- these topics are just too sensitive for most pastors. Good leader, ask yourself: would they be too sensitive for Jesus? Of course not. He'd speak out. So should we. So should you.

You live Christian discipleship when you work within your church to nudge it closer to Jesus. St. Paul challenged the church to welcome Gentiles, and to not require them to be circumcised, as Jewish law stipulated. St. Augustine made Christian theology coherent to the masses, and then modeled the disciple's path by publicizing his Confessions. For all his imperfections, Martin Luther stood up to (and eventually cleaved from) a misguided Catholic Church. St. Francis, St. Clare, St. Ignatius of Loyola, St. Benedict– all opened the church's doors and windows so fresh winds could blow in. So too with Mother Teresa, Corrie Ten Boom, Martin Luther King, Dorothy Day and many more.

Today, too many Christian churches are frozen. Who will lead them closer to Jesus? Disciples: that's what our churches need.

Discipleship starts on the inside; it progresses outward. The more we learn about Jesus, the more we are drawn into a reflection upon the state of our soul. Soon, without even realizing it, a change arises within us. We begin to hold ourselves to a higher standard. We find ourselves trying to "do what Jesus would do" in more situations. We begin to look beyond ourselves; to widen our circles of care. All of this helps prepare us to evangelize with our lives— to find a friend, be a friend, and bring a friend to Christ. Within the church and beyond its walls.

We go to church to receive encouragement and be challenged on our soul journeys. But it's a two-way street. Just as every church is called to challenge us, so we are called to challenge the church. For every church is *also* on a soul journey. Every church is a human construct, guided by God but influenced by history, culture and human power dynamics. A church is at its best when it seeks to understand and convey Christ's love, truth, grace and call. When a church is not at its best, leaders of goodness must rise up and act. Yes, good leader, you go to church to grow and learn-- to advance your own soul journey. But you also attend so as to make your church better. This requires that you question, challenge and, when necessary, nudge your church back towards Jesus.

No disciple is perfect. As the Roman centurion said to Jesus, "Lord, I am not worthy that you should enter under my roof. But only say the word, and my soul shall be healed." (Luke 6: 6-7). Even so, Jesus can work miracles with modest tools. He seeks our intention, not our perfection. To every imperfect disciple, His call is the same: "Love Me. Love others as you love yourself. Go out into the world. Build fellowship. Teach. Stand out; be steadfast and courageous. Deny yourself. And most importantly, imitate Me in all you do, to the best of your ability, every day." He gives the same call to His church.

No matter how hard we try, of course, we (and our churches) are sure to fall short. But if we love Jesus and seek Him always, if we surrender all to His will, perhaps we might, as the sick woman did, "touch the hem of His garment". And that is enough.

If you are a church leader, you bear an awesome responsibility. Whether clergy or lay minister, you are an instrument of God. You are called to carry Christ's message to the flock– both in your words and your deeds. You are called to make your church more loving at its heart, and more serving and welcoming at its fringes. If the flock sees leaders who are humble, gracious and filled with love, they will respond accordingly. If not, they will become lost and in the shadow of death. That's why, before you accept a leadership role, it is so vital for you to do the deep soul work necessary to become a disciple.

Are you one? Are you ready? Will you lead?

Next week, my letter to you will explore the topic of race relations.

"Just as there are many parts to our bodies, so it is with Christ's body. We are all parts of it, and it takes every one of us to make it complete, for we each have different work to do. So we belong to each other, and each needs all the others."-- Romans 12: 4-5

Yours in discipleship,

Tom

Week 38 -- Community: Race

TOWARDS A CLIFFTOP FLAG

Next step, free solo, towards a clifftop flag,
though footholds crumble– rainfall spurs the slip–
she climbs against a downward-pulling drag
that wants to hold her color in its grip.

Up sediment layers of bigotry's cost,
scraped she climbs. Faith defeating gravity,
courage summoned to leap the cross,
raw she climbs. Defiant strong; past history.

You who stand at top: what flies from hand?
Is that a stone you cast, or is it rope?
Are you the rock this climber must withstand?
Or are you one rappelling line of hope?

No matter which, she'll make it on her own.
But blessed is the rope, and cursed the stone

Rising Leader,

At 12:03 AM on July 21, 2022, my first grandchild was born. Maddie Mohr. She is perfect, and I am a goner. She's such a little thing– light as a whisper– with a shock of hair and the tiniest features on her angelic face. She has quickened my heart, giving me fresh impetus to write you these letters. I can't help but imagine her future. It is my most fervent prayer that my generation and yours will find some way to pass on to her generation a healing world.

To heal this world, we must heal our communities. To heal our communities, God calls us to see with new eyes. We who 'have' are called to see the hardships– and the trauma– of the many who 'have not'.

I was born in 1955. At ten years old, in 1965, I was sent to Camp Dudley in Westport, NY for the first of eight summer seasons. Camp

Dudley is the oldest boys' camp in North America (it now also has a separate girls' camp), and attracts a privileged kids crowd. At the time it also featured a scholarship program that gave a free ride to kids from disadvantaged communities. The program still exists today.

At Dudley, campers were organized into cabins. Each cabin held about eight kids. We spent a lot of time with our cabin mates—including at mealtime. It was on the first full day at camp, while at lunch with my freshly-introduced ten- and eleven-year-old cabin mates, that I experienced my first consciousness of race difference. We were together at our table for lunch. Just one orange was left, and three boys wanted it. So I began a rhyme, pointing from one to the next: "Eeny meeny miny moe…" At that moment, Larry Williams shouted out: "No!" I had thought to finish the rhyme with "catch a 'tiger' by the toe", but realized at that moment that a racist word had once lived inside that rhyme.

Larry was from Harlem. He knew racism; it was part of his daily experience. Sitting at lunch that day, having just met his cabin mates, he had the courage to call it out. I remember feeling mortified. I turned beet red and shrank into my shell as the other boys shifted awkwardly in their seats. But how did Larry feel? I know I didn't apologize to him. Larry, if you're reading this letter now, I'm sorry for what I said.

Larry and I returned to Dudley each summer. We fished together, we competed in sports. About five years after that event, I happened upon Larry sitting with a camp counselor. He had approached him to learn about a military career. This counselor had been in the Navy; as I stood there he said to Larry something like, "Well there is prejudice everywhere, but I do think the Navy is better than the other services in keeping the door open for Blacks to rise in rank." It hit me then, and it does now over fifty years later, that every day of Larry's life he dealt with the hidden acid drip of racism. It permeated everything.

Not so for me. The simple fact of my lighter skin pigmentation has saved me from a lifetime of snide comments, humiliating jokes, suspicious glances, wide-berth avoidance detours, doubts about my capabilities, and in-store clerk distrust. I've been given the benefit of the doubt at every turn– most recently when I was pulled over for an illegal traffic move, and was let go with just a warning. Privilege. It's a gift that keeps on giving. Racism. It's a curse that keeps on cursing.

Many of those who hail from European descent are sick and tired of the race conversation. Mentions of the history and legacy of slavery are met with "here we go again: the same old victim narrative". "I don't have an ounce of prejudice in me," some say. "Some of my best friends are Black (or Asian, or Native American, or Hispanic)." Yet the fight to protect the perquisites of prejudice rages. School boards have been overtaken by those intent on banning books and race conversations from schools. On television, talking heads promote "White Replacement Theory" while attacking "Critical Race Theory". Many can't say the phrase "Black Lives Matter" without adding "All Lives Matter", or "Blue Lives Matter."

We can't just cover our eyes and yell "yayayayaya" to avoid the truth. There is a hidden caste system that exists in our country. It reveals itself in that flash of anger when hidden rules are broken: an unspoken "look at her– she doesn't know her place". We see it in new encounters when our minds subconsciously conduct a "first sorting", a hierarchical judgment. We see it in the clerk who follows the Black shopper around; the joke about the Asian driver; the edging aside of the Hispanic woman from the outside-the-library girl gaggle during frosh orientation week at college.

As pervasive as caste is, it's like a broken calculator. It can't ascertain anything accurately– whether that be talent, character or threat. Yes, we are of many colors. We all fall somewhere on the pigmentation scale, ranging from dark to light, and in hue from yellow to red. Racial purity is meaningless: we all originated from Africa; we are all mongrels of varying shades– composed of a diverse array of racial mixtures, arising out of our fluid ancestries and genealogical histories.

More importantly, we are all equal in the eyes of God– interconnected and interdependent. What does God see when He looks upon humanity? He sees His children: each unique, each equally beloved.

So it should be with us, when we look upon each other. We are brothers and sisters– with hopes and dreams that in the end are more similar than different.

Privilege is an interesting word. Some privileges of wealth and status have been earned by hard work (mixed with God-given talent). Though let us never underestimate the degree to which accidents of birth have lent some of us advantage. I know that I stand on the shoulders of those who gave me an advantaged start. But then there are those privileges that are utterly unearned. Handed down wealth is unearned. Any advantage gained from skin tone is unearned. Just as those who suffer from unearned disadvantage have every right to fight for equity, so those who have privilege have every duty to do the same. Good leader, those of us who are privileged must learn to give privilege away.

How?

First, we admit it exists. We self-reflect upon our own unconscious biases, and work to banish them. And then we work to do the same in the world. We do not let racist comments go unchallenged. We recognize that the path to reconciliation begins with truth, and so we resist attempts to whitewash racism's history.

When we walk into a room, we don't just gravitate to those who look like us, those who command privileged attention. We seek out those who do not look like us, or who might hover at the edges. We see, we welcome, we inquire, we validate. In a situation requiring community leadership, we don't presume we must always be the one to lead. We stand aside; we support the other leader; we find reward in follower-ship. We enjoy the shared power of team diversity.

More important than anything else, we connect. We seek out encounters with those who look different from us. In new encounters, we skip lightly past our first visual instincts (with all their faulty calculations and baggage). We seek to learn about the real person in front of us– her hopes and dreams; his challenges and opportunities; his family; her friends.

Our communities are becoming ever more diverse. We can either see that fact as a threat, retreat to our tribal camps and mobilize the forces of evil to deepen the divide and buttress the rotting structure of caste; or we can see our neighbors with new eyes– embracing our equality of worth– celebrating our differences– rejoicing in our interconnectedness– and sensing the love of God interwoven in our midst. Which path is of God? Which will give joy? Which will you choose?

Next week, my letter to you will take up the topic of charity.

"There is neither Jew nor Greek, there is neither slave nor free, there is no male and female, for you are all one in Christ Jesus."-- Galatians 3:28

Yours in equity and inclusive encounters,

Tom

LETTERS TO RISING LEADERS

Week 39 -- Community: Charity

GOODNESS HIDDEN

Priest and Levite averted eye as passed
the sorely wounded, near-to-death Jewish man
It took a lowly foreigner outcast
to care and stop and kneel and lend a hand

He gathered him up, carried to hotel,
then overpaid for health to be reclaimed.
I wonder whether victim, when got well,
could even share with friends his helper's name?

My guess: this gentle act of charity
was carried out in anonymity
so healer and victim both might stay free
from victimhood, or pride, or vanity

Out of need's descent, you and he will rise
But more high's the lift if inner's the prize

Rising Leader,

Every act of charity is a gift to God. It plants a flower of goodness,
bringing beauty and healing to the world.

For years, a retired couple down the road has been dedicated to the
work of saving our planet. Another dedicated woman I know has, for
two decades, served as executive director of a food bank in Milwau-
kee. One man organizes a church group that brings Eucharist to the
homebound; another offers companionship to the dying. One
woman mentors disadvantaged youth in college prep courses;
another serves on a board of a charity that makes nature more accessible to inner city youth. The man who ran a 52-mile ultra marathon
on behalf of a charity that serves families of children with special
needs took two weeks to heal. Did you hear about the successful

woman executive who paid a restaurant in India to stay open during Covid, offering free meals to starving families?

One day we wake up, and realize life is not just about us. All people and things are interconnected, with love interwoven. As we contemplate the purpose of our lives, it hits us: we can be the love that interweaves, like the roots of a beautiful plant. Not the other guy– us. Not in some far-off land– right here. We can plant love right in our own community, rife as it is with need. Wounded though we are, we can step forward. We can take up the work. This is charity: our compassionate, God-guided response to the woundedness of the world.

In charity, we join hands with others on a shared journey of need. As is always true with love, it's relational, reciprocal. It's not a "handing down"; not a "better than". Jesus washed the feet of His disciples– an act of loving submission. To do so was a gift to Him, and to them. Charitable work enriches both giver and recipient, because charity is of God. Can you see how it flows up naturally from its foundation in piety, decency and civility? It's yet another step up the leadership ladder I like to call the "disciplines of goodness":

Charity brings cooling waters to a world aflame with need. Children need access to a better education. Food stamp recipients need jobs. Inner city kids need access to parks and nature. Parents of special needs children need resources. Shut-ins need companionship. Prisoners need hope. The sick need cures for horrible diseases. The dying need hospice care. An ailing neighbor needs a meal. Refugees need shelter. Villages need clean water; whole populations need food security. Our planet needs rescue. Who will meet these needs?

In the seesaw battle between life and death and good and evil, charity tilts– tipping the balance towards God and goodness. Closed doors are opened. Hungry mouths are fed. Imperiled lives are saved. Another soul finds hope. Some small part of the planet is healed. In tiny increments, soul by soul and act by act, we build a better world.

But where does the charitable urge come from? It emerges as a call from God, heard within the ready soul. The ready soul is not the perfect soul– such a soul doesn't exist. We can be selfish most of the time, but give sometimes. We can be caught up or weighed down, and still give. But it does require a heart widened in its circle of care. And that, good leader, takes interior work.

Each of us has our own unique soul journey. It culminates when finally we acknowledge our yearning for God. In that yearning, when at last we look around, we see Him. We realize He has been right beside us all along. He smiles and takes our hands. And then He leads us, step by step, back towards our original goodness. Our return is imperfect. We're still vulnerable in our gaps. But we're more mature, less naive, more leavened with knowledge. Our journey back to God and goodness prepares us to see beyond ourselves– to widen our circles of care– to give– to love.

This is the ready soul. As John Steinbeck said in *East of Eden*, "And now that you don't have to be perfect, you can be good." God hands us a flower, and asks us to plant it. We plant it so that we might restore, for some God-chosen part of the world, a glimpse of Eden. As we do, we soon discover we are not alone. God has placed flowers into the hands of billions. You and I, good leader, are just two planters in God's grand global garden. Each planted flower brings into the world more goodness, more love, more life. And the roots nourish and connect us all.

This is your mission. Return to God; make right your soul. Then go into the world to serve wherever He needs you– as a flower-planting giver, joining with your recipient in a reciprocal relationship of love– for Him and only Him.

Today's letter is the thirteenth and final one for Q3 ("Where's the Need?"). The letters for Q4 begin next Friday; these final thirteen letters will take up the question, "What's My Call?".

"If you pour yourself out for the hungry and satisfy the desire of the afflicted, then shall your light rise in the darkness and your gloom be as the noonday." – Isaiah 58:10

In charity,

Tom

FOURTH QUARTER:

What's my Call?

Week 40 -- Chance

THIS TOO IS JOY

Best we not seek a predictable day,
for life's meaning is found in the detours
Every twist bequeaths its fruit, come what may
In the end, no matter what, joy endures

Even then. When huge clouds darken the sky
When you fight and bargain and scream out your "why"
'til at last you succumb with surrendered reply
as your dreams fly away in one long goodbye

This too is joy. Though wounded, joy persists
as God teaches lessons in each turn of fate
Keep hands ever open for fortune's wrapped gifts
Once received, hand them on to those who await

How responds joy to the rolled dice of chance?
Joy trusts: to grow, to love, to give, to dance

Rising Leader,

When I was 9 years old, Mark, Paul and I went on a bike ride. My
bike happened to have a flawed braking system: when I back pedaled,
I could slow the bike down, but the action didn't lock the brake. It
just created friction, slowing the bike. So if I was going too fast it
took a long time to stop. Silly me– despite this flaw, I still thought a
long bike ride with friends would be a great idea.

We came to the precipice of a big hill. The dirt path down curved
into the woods; you couldn't see where it went. My friends talked me
into going first. As my bike picked up speed, I quickly realized I was
in trouble. I couldn't slow the bike. Two or three close calls with
trees later, I broke into a clearing. There before me was a bridge,
stretching over a creek. Well that's not quite accurate. The brick walls
lining both sides of the creek were there (the ones built to hold a

bridge). The bridge itself was not there. It was out.

And there was no way to stop. So my bike and I shot over the near side, flying into thin air above the creek. The brick wall on the far side caught my front wheel, pancaking it. I went careening over the handlebars. I must have been going fast, because my airborne body made it across and cleared the top of the brick wall on the far side. I remember seeing dirt, then sky, then dirt and sky again before I landed and tumbled to a stop, cut and bruised but not broken. It was a miracle I was alive.

Years later, in my junior year of high school, I joined friends at a big party at a classmate's parent-free home. The music was loud; the underage drinking was out of control. Somewhere deep into the night I heard some shouting. People began running towards the road in front of the house, and I followed. A body lay on the ground. As I stood there, an ambulance arrived. His name was whispered. It was a classmate of mine, lying motionless, covered in blood. I knew him well: someone not yet a close friend, but friendly to me. He had wandered too close to the road. A truck's rear-view mirror had hit him in the head and killed him. It was a horrific tragedy.

Chance. It marks the mundane and thunderbolt moments of our lives. Miracles. Tragedies. Unexpected encounters. Windfalls, shortfalls, pratfalls, pitfalls and downfalls. Where is God in it all? Why did He hand this one a winning lottery ticket? Why did He allow that one to suffer so?

God is omnipotent. But perhaps that just means He's poised for every possibility. Perhaps it doesn't mean God knows how everything will turn out, or that He predestined it. Because the whole idea of divine soothsaying and predestination gets in the way of free will, His great gift to His children.

Of course there are natural consequences— inexorable trends, predictable waves of change precipitated by behaviors and events. But God gives us freedom to choose our life path– all 7.7 billion of us. He doesn't master us as puppets; he waits and prays we will choose well. And since everyone and everything is interconnected, humanity's continuous and simultaneous free will choices interact with each other across time (in a stimulus / response way). As they do, they create a very large number of possible futures. Throw in the laws of nature (which explain the exact moment a rock dislodges from a hill and caroms down onto a bridge, or how certain cellular mutations create cancer in some people— that sort of thing) and the future's possibilities approach infinite.

All too often, as chance unfolds, we expect God to come to the rescue in the physical sense— to pull us right out of our calamities and crises and risky situations. When he doesn't, we lose faith. Maybe it's more helpful to see God as our ever-present soul-help in times of trouble. He is the One who loves us no matter what serendipities and tragedies rock and shock our lives. He is the Great I AM, always and intimately there: for us, with us, and in us. From life to death to life, forever and ever, Amen.

And if this is true, then it means our lives are not defined so much by the chance events we encounter, nor how God responds— but rather by how we respond. Do we turn to God? Do we share our sufferings and joys with Him? Do we trust His unfolding will? Do we seek out meaning, to discover any fruits the events of our lives might someday yield?

In our chance experiences, seeds of God's call are planted. A chance encounter with a homeless person might prompt an offer to buy a meal at McDonald's-- or strengthen our callous indifference. The loss of a child to random gun violence might prompt a parent to someday become an advocate for gun law reform-- or to die having never shaken paralytic despair. Winning the lottery might fund the building of a new community center-- or a life of gluttony. Every chance event in our lives offers us an opportunity to choose: will our hearts become smaller or bigger? Better or bitter?

Good leader, you are called to live a soulful life. To feel connected existence deeply, in all its joy and mystery. To trust God in every chance circumstance, knowing that peace and meaning will in time be found. God does not call us to be successful: He calls us to be faithful. We respond with all the love we can muster. Because in the end, love wins.

Next week, let's explore our consciences.

"I have said these things to you, that in me you may have peace. In the world you will have tribulation. But take heart; I have overcome the world."-- *John 16:33*

Here's to the God of Second Chances!

Tom

Song of the Month

PRAYER OF ST. FRANCIS

God my Father rule over my heart
Judge me gently
God my Father fuel the fire of my love
Forge me into a blessing

Make me a channel of your peace O Lord
Where there is hatred, help me love
Where there's offense, let me bring pardon O Lord
And where there's darkness, let me bring your light

Jesus Savior speak the truth I must know
Correct me, forgive me
Jesus Savior show the way I'm to go
Guide me, help me serve thee

Make me a channel of your peace O Lord
Where there's division, unify
Where there's despair let me bring hope O Lord
And where there's sadness ever joy

BRIDGE:

O Master, let me not seek
T be consoled but rather to console
To be understood, to be understood,
So much as to understand
As for love, sure let me seek it
But even more, let me give it
Teach me to give it

Holy Spirit storm your heavenly wind
Surround me, astound me
Holy Spirit form the words of my lips

Free me to speak like thee

For if I give I will receive
When I lose myself I'll be found
When I pardon I'll be pardoned
And when I die
And when I die
I'll be raised to eternal life

BRIDGE / Teach me to live it

Search for "Tom Mohr– Prayer of St. Francis"

To find this song on YouTube, Spotify and all music platforms

SHOW ME THE TRUE

One hateful comment sparks a hate-filled trend;
contagion grows in righteous fury spires.
One love-response to the hate and hearts bend;
Cool splash of water to quell raging fire.

Each day, our acts big and small bless or curse.
Choices are made in all we do and say.
Will we rise to better, or fall for worse?
Gather and grab, or give ourselves away?

Conscience, o conscience, return me back home
In God-centered guidance mark out His trail.
Before every response, whisper His poem,
so in my choices, the good will prevail!

Rule my conscience, Lord; show me the true
So I may forever only serve You

Rising Leader,

On any given day, we might choose the easy thing– to be our false selves, that confection we whipped up to "win" at the game of life. Falseness comes from a place of greed, envy, wrath, lust, gluttony, sloth or pride. Of course these motivations come well hidden– behind a camouflage of happy talk, false interest, bravado or a devil-may-care demeanor. In brief interactions, in the short term, we might get away with it. But if we act too often from our false selves, in time people will figure it out. They'll begin to expect us to act in a small-circle, all-about-us way. That's what it looks like when we keep God at arm's length.

Or we might choose to act from our true selves. Our true selves aren't camouflaged. What you see is what you get. The true self is what remains once the false self is stripped away– a free and naked soul. It lives in an authentic relationship with God and people. When we act from our true selves, we know we're imperfect. And so we take our choices to God. In the silence of our souls, we attend to that prick of conscience, the nudge that edges us ever closer to the good thing, the better choice.

But where does the conscience come from? It's interwoven into who we are as human beings– part of our original goodness. It needs curation and refinement, which can only happen through instruction. Parents teach us our first explicit moral code, through both word and behavior. We learn from our church's teachings, and from the Bible itself. Parents, church doctrine and Holy Scripture all bring rigor and richness to our moral sensibilities. They are important contributors to a well-developed conscience.

But in the end, handed-down rules only take us so far. In the crucible of choice, it is to God Himself that we must turn. We must mull over every choice with God by our side, seeking His guidance in prayer. Chances present choices. In choosing, we shape who we become. Richard Rohr says it this way:

> "If we can trust and listen to our inner divine image, our whole-making instinct, or our True Self, we will act from our best, largest, kindest, most inclusive self. There is a deeper voice of God, which we must learn to hear and obey. It will sound like the voice of risk, of trust, of surrender, of soul, of common sense, of destiny, of love, of an intimate stranger, of your deepest self. It will always feel gratuitous, and it is this very freedom that scares us. God never leads by guilt or shame! God leads by loving the soul at ever-deeper levels...."

The siren calls of our modern world are loud. "You can have it all." "Morality is what you make it." "Dress for success: impressions matter most." "Faster and cheaper means better." "If it can't be measured by science, it's not real." "I read it on the Internet, therefore it's true." It takes real discernment, in quiet prayer, to sift past the world's wisdom so as to find God's.

When we block out these siren calls and seek God, He helps us move beyond them and ourselves. We realize we exist in relationship with Him— and, by extension, with everyone and everything. This draws us into a form of love much bigger than before. We widen our circles of care. We sense His challenge: "Leader of goodness, go in faith to love and heal the world." And so, when next we encounter need, our hearts are ready for the moment– to hear God's call in the gentle nudge of our conscience. Out of our chance circumstances, the nudges of conscience lead us towards our call.

Our call might be to serve inside our own home. Or to serve within our existing workplace. Or in our church. Or to go into our community, our nation or the work of our planet. In our discernment, we let our consciences guide.

To be guided by your conscience is a life choice– a fork in the road. Turn to your conscience in all your choices, good leader. It will lead you to better decisions. The conscientious soul listens for His voice, then follows– no matter what. Choice by choice, you will unveil your true self and find your calling– and so become a blessing to the world.

Next week, we'll open ourselves to be challenged.

"The LORD came and stood there, calling as at the other times, "Samuel! Samuel!" Then Samuel said, 'Speak, for your servant is listening.'"— *1 Samuel 3:10*

In conscientious thanks,

Tom

Week 42 - Challenge

MOTHER DEER

A nature photo caught my heart today
Mother deer, split-second before leopard's teeth
Serene because her two fawns had run away
To save her own, her own life she'd bequeathed

She could have run much faster than the fawns
Instead, she stood– and waited for the fall
Cameraman cried when this brave Mom passed on
Then gave honor by sharing with us all

Mom had to make a choice in just a second
And so do we in every blink of life
Self-preserve and run? Or stand and reckon?
Daily decisions that cut like a knife

Our choices knit the fabric of our lives
May we live to give– not just to survive

Rising Leader,

Before we can respond to God's call to public ministry, private soul work is required. God can't deputize us to heal the wounds of the world until we are ready. This call to private soul work often comes packaged as an invitation– one that challenges our status quo.

1996 was a consequential year for me. I was 41– happily married, blessed with two seven-year-olds. I was rising in my career. My wife Pageen, the love of my life, was (and is) a devoted Irish Catholic. So going to church every Sunday was, for her, a given. Early in our marriage, she had helped me sort through the hurts of my youth. Drawn (with her encouragement) into a regular church-going habit, I had begun to reflect more deeply upon my relationship with God. But still, faith seemed to me to be just one more spoke on the wheel of life. God was not yet my hub.

Then came an invitation.

One cold January day on our way out of Mass at our local Catholic church, Brenda (an inspiring woman, overflowing with life, love and energy) came up and invited Pageen and me to join a small faith-sharing group she and her husband John were forming. It was part of a church-sponsored program called Christians in Search. Pageen and I agreed, and for six Thursday evenings in a row, ten of us congregated at Brenda's and John's home. Each week we'd read short Bible verses, and then answer questions– until, invariably, the conversation would burst wide open. What wonderful conversations they were– probing, questioning, searching.

Later that year, in May, I received another invitation. This one was from another church friend– Tim. A big Promise Keepers event was scheduled at the Minneapolis Metrodome, and he and a bunch of guys from our church were going. Would I like to come along? In the mid-nineties, Promise Keepers was a men's Christian revival movement at the height of its popularity. I decided to join them. 80,000 men attended that two-day Metrodome event. The six of us from our church were probably the only Catholics in the crowd. But still– the talks, the music and the presence of so many men seeking God and goodness– it all impacted me deeply. I didn't subscribe to every single thing Promise Keepers advocated. Nonetheless, most men who attended that event were sincere in their faith; most exhibited humility of heart and a desire to become better, more God-centered men.

I will never forget a moment late that Saturday afternoon. Sitting in the nosebleed seats looking around the stadium at 80,000 guys, I fell into my own thoughts. The song *Awesome God* was being sung on stage: "My God is an awesome God, He reigns from heaven above– with wisdom, power and love, my God is an awesome God." I found myself reflecting upon Him, and upon the mistakes of my life. I whispered a silent prayer in my heart: "God: forgive me." Instantly, the response came back, clear as day: "I forgive you." My first reaction was to reject what I'd just heard. But the "voice" repeated. "I forgive you!", it said. It was beyond my rational conception: a message of mercy direct to the heart from God Himself. As I grappled with what had just happened, knowing few would ever believe me, my heart filled with joy.

Then came September of that year. Pageen and I received another invitation– to attend a three-day weekend "Cursillo" retreat. You can only attend a Cursillo retreat once in your life. In Spanish, Cursillo means "short course". In this context, it meant a short course on Christianity. I wrestled with whether to participate– after all, I was an executive and family man with many responsibilities– but in the end, Pageen and I both decided to go.

In Cursillo, the men's weekend comes first– followed two weeks later by the women's weekend. As I arrived Thursday evening, I was introduced to my table mates (there were five similar tables scattered around the room). I sat down with them– the eight guys I'd be spending most of my time with during the retreat. Introductions began. There were no executives. My group included a call center worker, an FBI agent, a chiropractor, and a carpenter. "What am I doing here?" said my ego-voice.

The carpenter spoke up, his hand resting on his Bible (I hadn't brought a Bible). "God is everything in my life. Every morning in prayer, I read from this, and reflect on what God is trying to tell me. Then I try to live it." Arrogance and cynicism crumbled at my feet as it hit me: this guy gets it way more than I do. Come to think— Jesus was a carpenter. A picture formed in my mind (true story): my table mates and I were on a bus bound for heaven. They were sitting comfortably inside the bus. I was holding onto the back bumper, clinging by my fingernails.

My Cursillo retreat was a deeply humbling, inspiring, transformative experience. I have never been the same. From that weekend on, I have recognized that God is the very hub of my life– not just one of the spokes. In retrospect, I realize it took all three invitations to shift my heart– the Christians in Search faith-sharing group, the Promise Keepers event, and the Cursillo weekend. Each led to the next. Of course, time and again since 1996 I have fallen short of God's call. But I've always picked myself back up; I've always returned to Him— seeking His mercy and welcoming His embrace. And I hope I do so for the rest of my life.

Whether or not you've experienced a year such as my 1996, I hope you too have been challenged by angels bearing invitations. Invitations such as these call upon us to change— to move beyond our status quo's. They challenge us to dive into deeper waters. Do we accept? If we do, our apprenticeship begins. We surrender. We do the soul work. Day by day in prayer, study and action, we make ourselves ready to become the hands and feet of Christ in the world.

Good leader, are you ready to receive your private challenge, to prepare your soul for God's public call? A hurting world awaits-- in hope that you will answer your call and rise to the need.

Next week, my letter to you will ask you to consider how God is calling you.

"Rejoice in the Lord always. I will say it again: Rejoice! Let your gentleness be evident to all. The Lord is near. Do not be anxious about anything, but in every situation, by prayer and petition, with thanksgiving, present your requests to God. And the peace of God, which transcends all understanding, will guard your hearts and your minds in Christ Jesus."-- Philippians 4: 4-7

Yours in invitation,

Tom

Week 43 -- Call

FROM NIGHT TO LIGHT

I found more comfort in control than trust
Protecting my self-interest like a hawk
I counted the world unsafe and unjust
So drew my assets high atop a rock

Then sat upon my assets like a stone
Peering upon activities below
Until it struck me: I was all alone
Safe, secure, uninvolved, unloved, unknown

I looked up to the sky and saw the stars
And then looked down to valley's sprinkled lights
And then to darkness in my heart cast far
From life and love and friends on this dark night

"Dear God," I said, "I surrender. Here I am"
"Take me, remake me– then use me in Your plan!"

Rising Leader,

Let's work backwards. What happens when we die?

As a Catholic priest, Father Brendan McGuire has often been called by families of the dying to offer last rites. Over the years, it has been his privilege to be at the bedside of "well over one hundred people" as they passed from life to death. He shares that it has taught him the reality of Heaven through experience, more convicting than doctrine or belief alone could ever be. He describes it as follows.

A person on the verge of death may experience a period of lucidity– an awakening. They will look with love upon the family gathered round. They will take in the priest, finding comfort as the last rites are performed. Then, in Father Brendan's words, "after a long period of gazing upon their loved ones, their gaze will rise above us; they'll look past our shoulders. Their faces will begin to shine with joy. I've heard many call out a greeting to long-gone family members– 'Mama!', or 'Johnnie boy, Johnnie boy!', that kind of thing. As if these lost loved ones are reaching down from Heaven to take them home."

Rising leader, the door to Heaven is wide open to all of us. It's our final free will choice: to be welcomed into the arms of God at our deaths. Steve Jobs was known for many things, but not so much for his faith in God. However, his autobiographer chronicles that he did struggle with the reality and essence of God in the months leading up to his death. Jobs' sister gave the eulogy at his funeral. Towards the end of the eulogy, she shared that at his death, a number of family members were present. Here's what she said they heard:

"Before embarking, he looked at his sister Patty, then for a long time at his children, then at his life's partner, Laurene, and then over their shoulders past them. Steve's final words were OH WOW. OH WOW. OH WOW."

What if we were to know with absolute certainty, in the prime of our lives, that the Bible verse (1 Corinthians 2:9) was true: "No eye has seen, no ear has heard, and no mind has imagined what God has prepared for those who love Him." If we were to glimpse the true depths of God's love right now– not just at our deaths– how would we lead our lives differently?

I submit we would love God back, with all we've got.

And if God is in all people and all things, and if we who are Christian believe Jesus Christ is God, then Christ is in every person we meet. The poor, the hungry, the homeless– in all, we see the face of Christ. Christ is also in our children's children's children– those who will suffer the most severe effects of planetary degradation. Christ is in those privileged to live in a democracy, and in those on the verge of losing it. Those we agree with, and those we don't. Those living in peace, and those suffering and dying in the midst of war.

When we begin to see God in the face of the ones who stand before us, can we respond with anything other than love? Will we not experience deeply the call to devote our lives to advancing goodness in the world? Mother Teresa said it this way:

> "At the end of our lives, we will not be judged by how many diplomas we have received, how much money we have made or how many great things we have done. We will be judged by 'I was hungry and you gave me to eat, I was naked and you clothed me, I was homeless and you took me in.' Hungry not for bread– but hungry for love. Naked not only for clothing– but naked of human dignity and respect. Homeless not only for want of a room of bricks– but homeless because of rejection. This is Christ in distressing disguise."

Billions around the world, certainly including those who do not profess a Christian faith, pursue lives of goodness. And God loves us all. He understands all that led us to our beliefs. He celebrates our acts of goodness no matter what beliefs we might subscribe to.

For those of us who do profess a Christian faith, God asks us to prepare– to do the soul work. Jesus greets us first with love, then truth, then grace, and then, finally– call. We are called to become Christ's hands and feet in the world. To go where He would go, to do what He would do. His call to us flows up from our piety. Our piety connects us to God, and so draws us beyond ourselves and into the world. These are the steps up the ladder I call the "disciplines of goodness", which I've shared in past letters:

Loved one– child of the living God– rising leader. Which purpose calls out to you? Are you ready to rise up, take up the work, take a step up the ladder? With every step, your life becomes a greater blessing to the world.

Next week, let's turn to commitment. It's the way things get done.

"As He was going along by the Sea of Galilee, He saw Simon and Andrew, the brother of Simon, casting a net in the sea; for they were fishermen. And Jesus said to them, 'Follow Me, and I will make you become fishers of men.' Immediately they left their nets and followed Him."-- Mark 1: 16-18

Yours in calling,

Tom

Week 44 -- Commitment

STEP UP

If, when God asks for more than is convenient,
And claims some of the downtime of your day,
What depth will you reveal in your commitment?
Will you step up, or quiet fade away?

If, when all goes wrong, will you keep balance?
Will you trust in Heaven to get you through?
Will you turn to team and trust their talents,
When well-constructed plans are knocked askew?

If, when all is lost, you gather pieces
If you still stand when all have fled their posts
If from defeat you glean the things it teaches
And learn, and try again with your utmost

Then all might fail, or fruits might sprout emergent
Regardless: God will say, "Well done, My servant!"

Rising Leader,

Have you received and accepted God's call? Good. Now the real work begins.

For the past nine years, I have coached technology company CEOs. Most are backed by venture capital– a form of investment that is high risk / high reward. A number of the CEOs I coach today have been with me for years– some over five years. When I first began to coach them, their companies were quite early stage. Now their companies are scaling into global enterprises.

Venture capitalists are often asked what distinguishes the CEOs who "make it big" (the ones who have founded and built global, iconic enterprises) from all other founders. The most common answer is this: "The great ones never quit."

This is an important lesson for those who seek to respond to God's call. In the work you are doing for God, rising leader, how committed are you? Is your work in service of God's call a side project, one that you'll get to in your free time, if nothing else (like a golf game) gets in the way? Or is it a core commitment– an essential expression of who you are– something you will prioritize at or near the top of the list?

I want to be clear. I don't subscribe to the notion that "you are what you do". You're a child of God. You have worth and dignity independent of your work. However, how we spend our time is a strong indicator of our priorities. If a meaningful part of our week is dedicated to service, and if we are putting our hearts and souls into it, then our vocations are primary vessels of our self-expression.

The point is, it takes commitment. Commitment isn't hard to muster at the beginning. It's in the crucible of crisis that commitment comes into question. When the crisis hits, do you hit the escape button or put your head down and keep on working?

Good leader, you are called to do consequential things. Whether it be to serve in a charity, strengthen our democracy, advance diplomacy or help the planet achieve sustainability– the work you are called to do takes leadership. You'll need to name the problem, envision a solution, design it, architect it, build it, implement it, stabilize it, optimize it and scale it. You'll encounter all kinds of challenges along the way. Will you keep your nose to the grindstone, working through every problem that arises? Or will you fold like a cheap tent at the first sign of difficulty?

Most significant initiatives go through a leadership cycle that looks something like this:

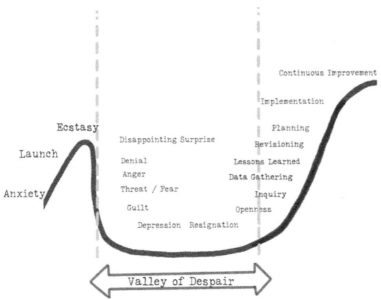

When everything falls apart, a leader has a choice– to stay or go. That's why a leader's depth of commitment can only be discovered in a crisis. When it hits, what does the leader do? Remember Ukrainian President, Volodymyr Zelenskyy, in the early days of the Russian invasion. US authorities were trying to help him get out of the country, to safety– so as to ensure continuity of government in the event (as everyone expected) Russian tanks were to roll through Kyiv. His response was, "I don't need a ride. I need ammunition." He chose to stay.

In these *Rising Leader Series* letters, I have spent much time writing about the work of our souls. It is in the encounters of our souls with God– expressed in love, truth and grace– that He prepares us for our call. In the apprenticeship of prayer, we untangle our soul knots and build up our resilience. So that when the crisis comes, we are ready to lean on Him for strength and stamina. We are sustained by trust and hope, recognizing that God has not asked us to be successful– He's asked us to be faithful. We know that if we wake up every day, if we take up the work at hand and do our best, we have done our part. The rest is up to Him.

How committed are you to your call? Will you give it your all? I pray you do– and that many years from now, as your life of service finally comes to an end, you will be able to look back and say, as St. Paul did, that you have "fought the good fight".

Next week, let's celebrate our gifts.

"For I am already being poured out like a drink offering, and the time of my departure is at hand. I have fought the good fight, I have finished the race, I have kept the faith. From now on there is laid up for me the crown of righteousness, which the Lord, the righteous Judge, will award to me on that day—and not only to me, but to all who crave His appearing."-- 2 Timothy 4: 7-9

Yours in commitment,

Tom

Song of the Month

THE PRISONER

He shares a cell, a two-bed cell, 20 hours a day
The other four hours he walks the yard, out of everyone's way
His soul is parched like a dying plant, shriveled on the ground
And his heart is cased in a ring of stone, a tall wall all around
Isn't he a discarded one, that we can just ignore?
Doesn't his past forfeit his right to expect any more?

Jesus says no, no, no
That man is my child
Won't you reach out, won't you reach out and love him?
Our Lord says no, no, no
Go rescue my child
There is no sin
That is greater than my love

But where do I start with a hardened heart who won't admit his
flaws?
He can't forgive what's been done to him nor forget the pain he's
caused
So why did you choose me to help? Aren't there others who could
serve?
Who am I to help this guy who got what he deserved?

Jesus says go, go, go
Your brother needs you now
Won't you reach out, won't you reach out and love him?
Our Lord says go, go, go
By the power of my love
I will choose you
To rescue my child

We are Jesus' hands and feet
If not us, then who?
I will be a servant of Christ. Will you join me too?

His Bible's new and his faith is young and he doesn't feel brave
But he's placed his past at foot of the Cross and by God's grace he's
saved
When you called on me to visit this man, I hoped you'd set him free
But I didn't know when you said "Just Go" what a change you'd
make in me

Jesus said go, go, go
And I found a hurting soul
And together, we made it back to Jesus

Our Lord says go, go, go
Go find my lost sheep
There is no sin
That is greater than my love
There is no sin
That is greater than my love
There is no sin
That is greater than my love

Search for "Tom Mohr— The Prisoner"

To find this song on YouTube, Spotify and all music platforms

Week 45 -- Gifts

OSCAR ROMERO

Romero was appointed archbishop
To toe the line in poor San Salvador
Everyone thought he'd keep low and kiss up
To the cloistered, wealthy benefactors

But in the city streets the poor were starving
The scent of revolution singed the air
In prayer before a cross-pierced Jesus carving
Romero heard a call to greater care

He went out, preached in soaring calls for justice
Despite the rising anger of the rich
Until at Mass when raising up the chalice
Assassin's bullet mixed Christ's blood with his

O God, what gift he laid at Your table!
Would I be so ready, willing, able?

Rising Leader,

When I was seven years old, I dreamed of becoming a professional football player. Quarterback sounded good at the time. But I had a small body with small hands, and wasn't particularly fast or agile or accurate. That dream died young. A few years later I found a tennis game, and dreamed of the professional circuit. But the folly of that dream was soon taught too, as I began to experience early exits from High School tennis tournaments.

Other gifts proved more promising. I did pretty well in school. I liked to read and write. I liked to act, to play guitar, and to write songs. In the college years, summer jobs helped me discover a knack for selling. After college, three friends of mine and I started a company that achieved some success. These early experiences were gift threads that

I drew upon to weave the tapestry of my career and life.

What are your gifts? Perhaps your parents glimpsed them in you when you were young. Some children show an early fascination with how trucks and machines and gadgets work. Others love to paint and draw, exhibiting unique talent in color combinations and forms. Others love to read, then learn to write at a young age– soon surprising parents with poignant poems. Athletic talent emerges early. So too the fascination with doctors and all things medical. One child sings beautifully; another dances with poise and grace. One is a social butterfly; another is quiet and contemplative.

Do our gifts come from nature or nurture? Nature wins, I think– at least in the beginning. We are each born unique, endowed by God with certain tendencies and competencies and quirks. Of course, our gifts must be developed. A gifted child with a paint brush will not become a successful artist unless she commits herself to years of dedicated training and effort. So it is with engineers, authors, doctors, singers, dancers, politicians and monks. Our gifts may arrive at birth, but what we do with them is up to us. And to develop them takes motivation.

Research shows that there are two types of motivation– extrinsic and intrinsic. Extrinsic motivation prods us from fear of punishment, or expectation of reward. Some people are stuck inside fear-based incentive systems-- living anxious, reactive lives. Others spend the better part of their lives chasing extrinsic rewards– the "hedonic treadmill". It's sad because it's a race that can never be won– there's always someone who has more– and it leaves the soul tired and empty. Intrinsic motivation, on the other hand, arises when what we do advances a purpose we care about, or feels like play, or promotes personal growth. Intrinsic motivation, once activated, tends to sustain– through thick and thin.

God gave us our gifts. And I believe it's important for us to ask ourselves: has the time come to give them back? There can be no higher purpose than serving God. The gifts God gave us are blessings to Him if– and only if– we put them to use for Him. When we use our gifts for God, we may experience "flow": that lost-in-the-moment, feels-like-play experience that comes when we do something we love. And of course, the more we exercise our "gift muscles", the more gifted we become. We grow. Purpose, play, personal growth– all come about when we give our gifts back to God. And progress begets confidence, which fuels our commitment and devotion– a virtuous cycle of goodness.

True confidence in our gifts is not of the ego. It is that salutary mixture of faith and hope that guides us forward. When we are confident, we trust in our God-given gifts, and that God will guide us in their use. Our minds clear as we focus on the task at hand. We keep a step or two ahead, anticipating all that emerges. No obstacle is insurmountable. We carry an inner certainty that with enough time and effort, we will overcome every challenge.

But in our consciousness of our gifts and mastery of our work, it is all too easy to make it about us– not about God. Pride: it's such an ever-present danger. Through prayer, through our soul-connection with God, we must work every day to bring all of our successes back to Him. In our gift-giving we are simply a contribution, one small part of something much bigger. All around us are those who seek to do the same. Together, we are the body of Christ– God's response to the world's hunger. For Him and only Him. St. Paul said it this way in 1 Corinthians:

> "Now there are varieties of gifts, but the same Spirit; and there are varieties of service, but the same Lord; and there are varieties of activities, but it is the same God who empowers them all in everyone. To each is given the manifestation of the Spirit for the common good. For to one is given through the Spirit the utterance of wisdom, and to another the utterance of knowledge according to the same Spirit, to another faith by the same Spirit, to another gifts of healing by the one Spirit, to another the working of miracles, to another prophecy, to another the ability to distinguish between spirits, to another various kinds of tongues, to another the interpretation of tongues. All these are empowered by one and the

same Spirit, who apportions to each one individually as He wills."-- 1 Corinthians 12: 4-11

The world cries out in need. Who will hear and respond? God has no hands and feet but ours. Will you use your gifts for just yourself, or will you return them to Him? It's your call. Your choice.

Next week, let's acknowledge (and even celebrate) our gaps.

"Now you are the body of Christ, and each one of you is a part of it."-- *1 Corinthians 12: 27*

Yours together in service to Him,

Tom

Week 46 -- Gaps

HUMBLE SCRAPS

I just spent twenty minutes with head bowed down,
seeking my God in contemplative prayer.
But mind hopped around like a rodeo clown
so much, I surely chased God out of there.

Or maybe not. Perhaps He still abided,
despite my discombobulated brain.
When intent and limitation collided,
perhaps He deemed intent the better claim.

Is this not the quintessence of our Savior?
That, knowing every wart and scar and sin,
notwithstanding frequent misbehavior,
yet still He calls for us to enter in?

Dear God, surprising lover of my gaps:
What goodness you create with humble scraps!

Rising Leader,

God willing, eventually the day will come when the desire of your
heart will rise, at last, to meet the call of your soul. When it does,
good leader, you will take up your mantle and step out into the great
beyond. As you do, you will bring your all– your whole being. Not
just your gifts– but also your gaps. Not just your wheat– but also
your weeds.

We are not perfect. If only I could do this thing. If only you could do
that thing. I wish I were more quick witted; you wish you were more
easygoing. I judge, gossip, flare up in anger; you pout. In the moment
of truth, you fail to do the charitable thing. In the crucible of conflict,
I shrink from the moment and lose courage. You suffer from shy-
ness, while I struggle with pride.

When Jesus first appeared to Simon the fisherman, revealing Himself as the Son of God, Simon's response was, "Go away from me, Lord, for I am a sinful man." Simon knew the measure of his gaps. Jesus responded by saying, "Come and I will make you fishers of men." Simon left his nets and followed Him. Sure enough, in the months and years leading up to the cross, Simon stumbled time and again. He was rash and impetuous; he was a slow-learning disciple. Nonetheless, at the appointed hour Jesus named him Peter (Peter means "rock"), and anointed him– saying, "Upon this rock I will build my Church." How Jesus' other followers must have reacted when, on the day He was captured and taken to the cross, Peter fled in fear. When confronted, Peter denied even knowing Jesus. What did the Apostles have to say about their appointed leader then? Three times. Three times he denied Him.

Yet Peter was chosen to become the first pastor of Christ's fragile, fledgling church. Starting with just ten apostles and a handful of other followers, he set the first roots of Christianity in the world. In the years after Jesus' ascension, Peter led the church as best he could. He stood up for the faith against the attacks of the Sanhedrin and the authority of Rome. He spoke with authority to the crowds. In the name of Christ, he healed the sick and the lame. He assigned disciples, guided communities and corrected sinners.

His leadership was also marked by mistakes. He didn't know what to do with the Gentiles– the non-Jewish followers– that Paul was converting. He was confused about whether they should follow Jewish law. Could Gentile Christians eat together with Jewish Christians? Did they need to be circumcised? It took him a long time to get to "yes" for the first question and "no" for the second. But he led as best he could, and the church grew despite his failings. Knowing his gaps as he did, he communed with God in constant prayer. He drew in other disciples and counted on them to do what he could not do.

Our gaps teach. They help us appreciate our dependence on God and others around us. We are not the "be all and end all". We are all simply contributions to God's great plan for humanity. All of humanity's greatest leaders were great in no small part because of (not despite of) their gaps. Mother Teresa's unrelenting doubt yielded humility and wisdom. Lincoln's lifelong struggle with depression shaped him into a clear-eyed realist, a sensitive and inspiring speaker and man ready to give all to the cause– including his life. Dag Hammarskjold's struggle with pride led him to a life of prayer and soul work that fortified his diplomacy. Imperfect leaders who keep close to God are both humble and authentic. Their very imperfections make them relatable, humanizing their leadership and sparking followership.

You are a work in progress, good leader. So am I. And it's OK. We are called to get in the game, do our best, and learn. This is the disciple's path: stumble-step, stumble-step forward toward the good.

Next week, let's explore how we might grow towards our true selves.

"I don't mean to say I am perfect. I haven't learned all I should, even yet, but I keep working toward that day when I will finally be all that Christ saved me for and wants me to be."-- Philippians 3: 12

Yours in imperfect service,

Tom

LETTERS TO RISING LEADERS

Week 47 -- Growth

NO ONE MOMENT

There was no one moment when I found myself.
Just a two-forward, one-back together-walk
with God. Words from soul; book prayers off the shelf.
Peeling away, sorting meaning, taking stock.

There was no one moment when I found my call.
Just nudges, senses of invitation.
Songs caught in the wind, asking for all–
me humming along in harmonic vibration.

I keep finding new we-truths: it never ends.
I keep hearing call songs: they draw me forth.
These days I mostly pray that I might spend
what's left of my life winding towards True North.

My God, may the roaring thunder of Your Heart
fill mine with the real; beckon me to my part.

Rising Leader,

The Bible says God created heaven and earth in just one week. Quite
a week! But what happened the week after that? Our Creator kept on
creating. Out of the past and into our now, God's creative power sustains– a continuous rolling thunder of love. He created you and me,
sending us into the world for this time. Here we will remain, until life
yields to death, then yields to new life with God forever. If we were
to ask ourselves what our mission is in the meantime, on Earth, I
think we could agree that it is to grow towards Him. We grow
towards Him by growing into our true selves. We grow towards Him
by growing into our purpose.

How do we grow into our true selves?

As we rise from childhood to adulthood, we learn the world's values. We see what yields status. We see what yields fortune. We see what the world calls normal. We sense what is expected– from parents and friends and colleagues. Accordingly, in our bid to fit in, or measure up, or rise above, or look down upon, we construct our ego– the face we wish to present to the world. It incorporates our gifts, but hides our gaps. It conveys some preferential mix of faux happiness and faux confidence. This is our false self.

But over time, it gets old. It begins to drain us. It becomes harder and harder to keep up the appearance: each day to paint the face, each day to perform the false self's magic tricks. Until, perhaps triggered by an event, in the surprise of a deep-dive relationship with the One who loves us most, we let go. We suddenly see that we don't need to wear this heavy mask anymore. We are good, just the way we are. We can return to our essence– to our imperfect, true selves. It takes time. It's a journey. But whether we embark on it in our twenties, or thirties, or fifties, or seventies, no matter. Each and every step towards the truth of our being is growth.

How do we grow into our purpose?

Victor Frankl was a Viennese psychiatrist. In 1942 he was captured by the Nazis and thrown into a concentration camp for the crime of being Jewish. He suffered horrific abuse, and witnessed mankind's worst. After the war, he wrote (over a nine-day period) a book, *Man's Search for Meaning*, published in 1946. It became an international best-seller.

While on a book tour shortly after its publication, he was interviewed on TV in front of a live audience. The host asked him, "Mr. Frankl, you were captured by the Nazis and taken to the concentration camps, where you lived for three years, with suffering and death all around you. You witnessed the most terrible acts. You endured unspeakable maltreatment by the guards. How did you survive?"

Frankl paused and said, "I survived because I realized I was responsible." Gasps rose audibly from the live audience. "But what do you mean?" said the host. Frankl responded, "Let me explain more clearly. I finally realized that I was 'response-able'. In the space between every act of the guards and my reaction, I had the freedom to decide. Would I live in hope or fear? This choice was the only freedom I had. And once I realized I had that freedom, I knew I could endure."

Frankl's hope while in the concentration camps was to reunite with loved ones after the war. But in a larger sense, it was that someday he would have the opportunity to live out his life's purpose– to live long enough to give something back to the world, some enlightened response to all the darkness he'd experienced. At the time, under the thumb of the Nazi guards, he may not have fully understood that his life's meaning and purpose would be found in teaching others how to find meaning in their own lives. But he knew God had a call in store for him– and that he needed to endure the war, so he could live it out. He prayed daily and knew sacred scripture. Perhaps he was consoled by Deuteronomy 31:6: "Be strong and courageous. Do not fear or be in dread of them, for it is the Lord your God who goes with you. He will not leave you or forsake you."

Can purpose survive hardship? We do not get to set the ratios of our lives– our mix of sickness or soundness, triumph or tragedy, suffering or sufficiency. If we center our lives solely in pleasure or fame or financial success, then our "happiness" will be tethered to the twists and turns of our fortunes. Even then, will we be happy? But if we see life as a gift to be given back to God and to others, circumstance will hold less claim over our joy. God-guided purpose will stake the better claim. Said Frankl:

> "We who lived in concentration camps can remember the men who walked through the huts, comforting others, giving away their last piece of bread. They may have been few in number but they offer sufficient proof that everything can be taken from a man but one thing: the last of the human freedoms – to choose one's attitude in any given set of circumstances, to choose one's own way…

The way in which a man accepts his fate and all the suffering it entails, the way in which he takes up his cross, gives him ample opportunity – even under the most difficult circumstances – to add a deeper meaning to his life."

It takes soul work. The secret to growth is not in what happens to us, but in how we respond. If we recognize that God eternal is with us every moment along our short journey upon this Earth, and that He loves us beyond all understanding, then we can handle all that life brings. In our times of suffering, we will grow in sensitivity and humility. In the surrender that occasions our failures, we will hand our egos over to our God, to do with them what He will. And in our times of success, when we have caught the wave of life at high tide, we will do our best to remember it is all for Him. He is our meaning. He is our hope. He is our joy.

The quest of our lives is to find our authentic selves and our reason for being. Together, these are the holy grail we most seek, for they are God in us. God in our being, and God in our doing. Everything that happens to us along the way– the good, the bad and the ugly– is an occasion for growth. We can learn and grow from everything: from our sins, our wounds, our broken hearts, our mistakes and failures. As Frankl said, it's our choice.

The world counts on you to go and grow, good leader. Into our wounded world you must go, true to yourself and fueled by the fire of His call. Trust that as you do, you will grow by every experience. God will use every life event to draw you ever closer to His light. As you take up your call to leadership– as you assemble your team, as you rise from a doer, to a coach of doers, to a coach of coaches– God will be by your side. Grow with Him towards your truth and His goodness, good leader, as a flower towards the sun. Only in God is your soul at rest. Only in God will you find your truth and a meaning worthy of all you have to give.

Next week is Thanksgiving. May you be the gift this world needs. Praise God, from whom all blessings flow. Praise Him, all creatures here below. Praise Him above, ye heavenly host. Praise Father, Son, and Holy Ghost!

In my letter to you next week, I will take up the topic of grace, by sharing "the rest of the story".

"When I was a child, I talked like a child, I thought like a child, I reasoned like a child. When I became a man, I put the ways of childhood behind me. For now we see only a reflection as in a mirror; then we shall see face to face. Now I know in part; then I shall know fully, even as I am fully known."-- 1 Corinthians 13: 11-12

Yours in truth and call,

Tom

LETTERS TO RISING LEADERS

Week 48 -- Grace

HAL LANCE'S SONG

A stroke cost Hal facility to speak
Except in raspy, out-of-kilter blurts
Each step confessed a hard-won new technique
Carried with gentle grace that clothed his hurts

He'd joined the team that led our men's retreat
Diminished though he was, his faith was strong
On Day Three, when program called for music sweet,
Hal broke, a cappella, into song

"Here I am, Lord. Is it I, Lord?" he squeaked
The most perfect aria we'd ever heard
It pierced our hearts so deep, it made us meek:
Awestruck, opened, and ready for God's word

Abba, thank you! For the angels that you send
Who sing into our hearts the notes that mend

Rising Leader,

What is grace? Grace is God's undeserved favor and His ever-guiding hand. My wife Pageen describes it as "that which God does within us, without us." God grants us His grace because of who He is– not who we are. But then it turns to us to respond. Will we take God's grace for granted? Or respond with gratitude and service?

Perhaps the Bible's best-known story on the subject of grace is the parable of the Prodigal Son. In it, a father has two sons. The younger son demands that his father give him his inheritance immediately– not, as it should be, after he dies. The father acquiesces. The son immediately takes the money, flees his home, and spends everything in dissipation. Coming to his senses, he slinks back home, hoping his father might let him work with the pigs in return for food.

But when the son crests the hill, the father sees him. He runs to his son, wrapping his arms around him. He orders servants to get new clothes and to prepare a feast. The older son hears the commotion, wondering what's going on. When he hears that his brother has returned, and that his father has thrown a banquet, the older son becomes angry. "I've served you all these years, and you've never given me a party," he says. The father responds, "my son, everything I have is yours. But your brother was dead and has come back to life. He was lost and now is found."

Many great sermons have been spoken on this parable— what we can learn about God, and how we might see ourselves in the younger son, the older son and even in the father. But I've never heard anyone talk about the sequel— what happened next. Yet, isn't "what happened next" the most important thing? Isn't this the most important question for us: how will we respond to the exuberant grace of God?

Please allow me to imagine with you the rest of the story.

In the days after the banquet, the younger son couldn't shake his shame. Caught in the grip of selfish compulsion, he had committed the gravest possible insult by demanding his birthright before his father's death. And then he'd wasted it all. What remaining claim could he have to his father's or his brother's love? The coldness of his brother was almost a consolation, because it was what he felt he deserved. But his father's love overwhelmed. He couldn't square it with what he had done. Each morning, the father greeted him with a hug. Each morning, the younger son hung his head. Until one day, the father asked that he join him for a walk in the field.

They walked in silence for a time, until the father turned and said, "Why do you reject my gift?" The younger son looked up, his face etched in pain. "Father, what I did— it cannot be forgiven. I will never be worthy of your love." The father took his shoulders in his hands. "My son, look at me. Do you love me?" "Yes, father, you know I love you with my whole heart." "Then why will you not let me love you?" "I am not worthy." "Son: answer me. I will not ask again. Will you please accept the love I have for you?" The son looked into his father's kind eyes for a long time, and tears began to flow. "Yes, father. If you will love me even as I am, even though I have done what I have done, then I will forgive myself. I receive your love right now, with gratitude. With joy!"

A new routine took hold. After morning prayers with his father and brother, the younger son dedicated himself to the work of the farm. Each day he strove to lighten the others' burdens. His brother remained cold and distant, but he understood. One day while in the field, he heard his older brother call out. "Come quick! Father has fallen." The younger son ran across the field, joining his brother at the side of their father, lying on the ground.

The stroke stole his voice and the use of his left side. The younger son took up the task of feeding and caring for his father. Whereas before the stroke his father had led morning prayers, now he did. Whenever his father slept, he completed whatever farmyard chores he could. Months went by, until one morning, while washing his father's face, he felt a tight grip upon his arm. His father pulled him down with unexpected strength, bringing his own face inches away. His father lifted up his head just enough, and kissed the younger son on the cheek. And then he died.

The father's entire estate went to the older son, as was his due. The younger son came to his brother and said, "I am sorry that I hurt you, dear brother. You were the one who stayed and served father, keeping the farm while I ran away. This farm is now yours, and it is time for me to make my life elsewhere. Know that I will always love you." The older brother's face remained cold and impassive. The younger brother smiled sadly, took what possessions he could carry, and went on his way.

The older brother married and raised five children. One day a traveler stopped by, bringing news about his brother. He lived in a city two days' journey away. He worked in service of the poor. He lived on the generosity of strangers. The next day, the older brother left in search. The younger brother was no longer young. The day was warm and bright as a small crowd gathered around him in the town square.

Helpers were there to pick up food packets, prepared for the poor and homebound. He stood by a table, assigning the volunteers their packets and visits.

As he looked up, he saw a figure in the distance, walking down the street in his direction. Somehow the silhouette looked familiar. In a squint, he recognized his older brother. With a cry, he dropped everything. He ran, stumbled, and ran again, arms reaching out. "My brother," he said. "How I've missed you." They hugged as his older brother wiped the tears from his eyes and whispered, "I love you. I forgive you. Please forgive me."

And that is how the story ends.

Good leader, how will you respond to God's grace? Will you take up your cross and follow Him wherever He leads? Will you become a leader of goodness, making a difference and giving to others the grace you have received?

Next week, let's stoke the fire.

"And now I commend you to God and to the word of his grace, which is able to build you up and to give you the inheritance among all those who are sanctified."--Acts 20:32

Yours in grace and gratitude,

Tom

Song of the Month

MOTHER MARY, ORDINARY

Mother Mary
Ordinary
Called to carry
The Child of God

Though you couldn't perceive
What God could conceive
You said let it be done to me
According to thy will

CHORUS:
Where does your strength come from?
What kind of love is this?
That made you Mother of our God?

SPOKEN:
As a baby, Jesus was comforted by lullabies sung by a loving mother
In time, he grew in wisdom and stature
And then, at the appointed hour, he went into the world
To proclaim the good news
To heal the broken and to save souls
Until he was betrayed by a kiss
And began his Passion
His mother close by at every step

Mother Mary it must have been scary
To see your son carry
That cruel wooden Cross

But you stood by that tree
And witnessed the deed
And watched your Son bleed
As a ransom for souls

LETTERS TO RISING LEADERS

CHORUS

Mother Mary come to me, come to me
Teach me your courage and your faith
Mary gentle, Mary kind, Mary strong
When Jesus came to dance, you were his song

What lullabies
Did you sing when He cried?
Did you sing as He died?
And the world turned dark?

And then when he rose
What songs must have flowed
From your heart of gold
As the world gleamed in light?

CHORUS

Mother Mary come to me, come to me
Teach me your courage and your faith
Mary gentle, Mary kind, Mary strong
When Jesus came to dance, you were his song
When Jesus came to dance, you were his song

Search for "Tom Mohr– Mother Mary, Ordinary"
To find this song on YouTube, Spotify and all music platforms

Week 49 -- Fire

MISSIONARY'S EULOGY

We stand by your casket– remains of the Earth
Your life just a memory– carried treasure
For forty years you stayed, honored our worth
Giving us, the forgotten, you last full measure

Can poverty's heartbreak be closed just with care?
Can one person's acts turn want on a dime?
Perhaps not. But lived love does lessen despair
You saw us, walked with us, hand-helped our climb

And now we are left with one heart-gaping hole
In this place, we will always honor your name
You lived by God's grace, with fire in your soul
Which set ours alight in perpetual flame

"Thank you" seems tiny, when you warrant best
We love you– we'll miss you– by you we were blessed

Rising Leader,

Climate change… war… threats to democracy… racial strife… poverty… hunger. The crises of our time are beyond easy answers. It's so easy to inch past the crash scene, rubbernecking but not stopping to help. Alarmed but unmoved. If "not my problem" echoes in our minds, our hearts are sure to harden. And each time we drive away, we will diminish ourselves. We will become more self-centered; our dreams will be smaller; we'll feel more fearful. Until we find ourselves shrink-wrapped, in the words of Henry David Thoreau, into "lives of quiet desperation".

Is this our lot? To spend our short time on Earth caught in a dwindling circle of care, endlessly fretting as we wait for the next shoe to drop?

God says no. In love, He reaches out to our hearts. He asks that we trust Him. He assures us that, with His help, we will find ourselves. We will see our goodness, will see the need around us, and will be inspired to advance the good. God wants us to live heroic lives; to dream the impossible dream. Hearts set to light, we will then be released like floating lanterns by God, to become light for the world.

God needs leaders on fire-- leaders who burn with desire to make a difference. Leaders who stare down the crisis or need or injustice, and do not shrink. Who will work for the good, against all odds. So that through us, God might renew the face of the Earth.

In the play *Man from La Mancha*, Don Quixote heads off on a quest to restore chivalry, battle all evil, and right all wrongs in the world. Everyone he meets sees him as a lunatic, caught up in fantasy, a deluded idealist. He and his sidekick Sancho soon come to a roadside inn. Don Quixote is convinced it's a castle. While sitting at a table, he notices a gang of men propositioning a server, who is also a prostitute. Her name is Aldonza, but Don Quixote is convinced she is the princess Dulcinea: a fair lady of great dignity and worth. He rises to her defense, stepping between her and the men and proclaiming her virtue. Aldonza becomes confused and angry. When later she confronts him, she calls him an irrational old fool, describing herself as just a prostitute. But he insists again she is a lady, due great honor and respect. For the first time she sees herself through his eyes. She begins to believe. When she asks where he is going, and why, he sings the song, *The Impossible Dream*.

To dream the impossible dream– to fight the unbeatable foe
To bear with unbearable sorrow– and to run where the brave dare not go
To right the unrightable wrong– to love pure and chaste from afar
To try when your arms are too weary– to reach the unreachable star

This is my quest–to follow that star– no matter how hopeless– no matter how far
To fight for the right– without question or pause
To be willing to march into Hell for that Heavenly cause

Time and again throughout history, leaders of goodness have risen up, hearts ablaze, to do the impossible.

Greta Thunberg is a leader on fire:

> "Adults keep saying: 'We owe it to the young people to give them hope.' But I don't want your hope. I don't want you to be hopeful. I want you to panic. I want you to feel the fear I feel every day. And then I want you to act. I want you to act as you would in a crisis. I want you to act as if the house is on fire. Because it is."

She has inspired millions of people to become more engaged in the fight to heal our planet.

Winston Churchill was a leader on fire. At the lowest point of World War II, after the fall of Dunkirk, when Nazi victory seemed inevitable, he said to the British people:

> "We shall go on to the end, we shall fight in France, we shall fight on the seas and oceans, we shall fight with growing confidence and growing strength in the air, we shall defend our Island, whatever the cost may be, we shall fight on the beaches, we shall fight on the landing grounds, we shall fight in the fields and in the streets, we shall fight in the hills; we shall never surrender."

And the people rose to their leader's challenge, and fought, and won.

Martin Luther King was a leader on fire. He said at the Lincoln Memorial:

> "Let us not wallow in the valley of despair.... Even though we face the difficulties of today and tomorrow, I still have a dream. It is a dream deeply rooted in the American dream. I have a dream that one day this nation will rise up and live out the true meaning of its creed: We hold these truths to be self-evident, that all men are created equal."

And he changed America.

Good leader, what is your heavenly cause? What sets your heart afire? Our world is in desperate need of heroes. Not in the military sense so much as leaders who live purpose-driven lives. Whether it be in your home, your community, your country or your planet, you are called to be heroic. To go into the broken world, fueled by the fire of His love.

Perhaps you will achieve the impossible. Or not– sometimes windmills stay windmills. Regardless of the outcome, God treasures your struggle for goodness. Your job, good leader, is to be heroic. The rest is up to Him.

"He only is my rock and my salvation, my stronghold; I shall not be shaken. On God my salvation and my glory rest; the rock of my strength, my refuge is in God."-- Psalms 62: 6-7

Yours by the fire of His love,

Tom

Week 50 -- Fuel

CHRISTMAS IN ME

One day, my Dad led my siblings and me
(With mist from our lungs afloat in cold air)
Up hill, toboggan-swoosh, in search of a tree
To the top, to find the perfect one there

With cut of the ax, the pine tree was felled
With grunting and pulling, sled slid through snow
Back to our car, where we laughed and we yelled
As Dad wrestled ropes as tight as would go

At home, we delighted when Christmas tree rose
Adorned it with ornaments, popcorn and such
Until, with a flourish, Dad said, "Here goes!"
And he stretched to place star, then adjusted a touch

Star-studded mem'ries, decked in childhood glee.
Will you show me, Lord, how to live Christmas in me?

Rising Leader,

The moment is now. God needs you to spark a movement that, in
some small way, will change the world for the better. It will take
work; you'll need followers and resources. But more than anything
else, it takes love.

How do you spark a movement?

Soul by soul. Just begin; you'll learn as you go. Keep your eyes peeled
and your heart open to the workings of the Holy Spirit. Perhaps
someone will notice what you're up to, and join you in the work. By
this approach, soul by soul, step by step, if it is God's will, your
movement will grow. Mother Teresa describes it this way:

"I never look at the masses as my responsibility. I only look at the individual. I can love only one person at a time. I can feed only one person at a time. Just one, one, one. You get closer to Christ by coming closer to each other. As Jesus said, 'Whatever you do to the least of my brethren, you do it to me.' So you begin... I begin. I picked up one person. Maybe if I didn't pick up that one person, I wouldn't have picked up the others. The whole work is only a drop in the ocean. But if we don't put the drop in, the ocean is one drop less. Same thing for you. Same thing in your family. Same thing in the church where you go. Just begin... one, one, one."

That's how you spark a movement.

When I began this series, I asked you to reflect upon three things: the state of your soul, the state of the world around you, and the call of your heart. It was my hope that in contemplation, you might be inspired to draw closer to God– and then to act. To step up and serve as a leader of goodness. Our world is unraveling at the seams; it pines for ethical leadership. Only gifted, dedicated, ethical leaders can stitch humanity back together.

Now, as this series draws to a close, my purpose remains the same. It is my fervent prayer that you will befriend God, work with Him to untangle your soul knots, listen for His call, fly to the need and become a contribution. Never underestimate the power of faith. God is everywhere. He sings to you from every rock and leaf. He calls to you from every wisp of wind. He loves you. He believes in you. He will clothe your life with meaning. He will help you move beyond yourself. He will help you open your heart, your arms, your calendar and your wallet to change the world.

The moment is now. You are tomorrow's leaders. Keys to the future are being handed to you and others in your generation. Will you use them to open yourself to greater love? Pray– with your whole self– to sense and follow God's guidance. Find a point of impact that you are uniquely designed to lead. Take up the cause, spread your message, and inspire others to join in.

The moment is now. For you are God's fuel. You brighten the fire of God's love in every act of goodness. Your spark lights a lantern in the darkest place. It burns down the walls of bigotry and injustice, raises the watchfire of consciousness, and turns hate into ashes and smoke. Who else but you? Your hands– your feet– your heart– your love. You (and those you bring along) are the ones called to sustain the fire of His love in the world.

This is the fiftieth letter in this *Rising Leader Series*. Just two letters remain. Allow me to offer you a few simple words to live by, words first shared in the Introduction to this book. It all comes down to this:

> *Leader of goodness,*
> *Go in faith*
> *To love and heal the world*

The moment is now. Act for the good. Love exuberantly, one soul at a time. Only for God, His people and His world.

"And the word was made flesh and dwelt among us. And we saw the glory of it, as the glory of the only begotten Son of the Father, which word was full of grace and truth... And of his fullness we have all received, even grace for grace. For the law was given by Moses, but grace and truth came by Jesus Christ."-- John 1:14-17

Yours (just one more twig of kindling for God's holy fire),

Tom

LETTERS TO RISING LEADERS

Week 51 -- Fear

FEAR'S REPLY

Does your life-light shine bright into the darkness?
Or is it blocked by the sum of all your fears?
Never let doubts be traitors to goodness
You were born to give your all for these short years

Though arrows dart by day all around you,
Though flames of fear come flying 'round the bend,
God Himself stands resolute beside you
Turn. Take His hand. Embrace the Great Amen

He's the One. Go seek His exhortation
A world consumed in need awaits your lead
Go chase with courage heavenly ambition
Submit, let God, let love become your creed

Surrender renders deeper piety
So hand fears to God; He'll carve your legacy

Rising Leader,

What are we to do with fear?

God chose a simple teenage girl from the countryside to be the mother of Jesus. While still betrothed to be married, the angel Gabriel came to her in a dream: "Do not be afraid, Mary, for you have found favor with God. And behold, you will conceive in your womb and bear a son, and you shall name Him Jesus."

What confusion and vulnerability Mary must have felt at those words. Overwhelmed, she asked, "How can this be, for I am still a virgin?" The angel's response could only have perplexed her further: "The Holy Spirit will come upon you, and the power of the Most High will overshadow you. For nothing is impossible with God."

Mary set aside her fears. She responded with the most important thing we can ever say when God calls and asks us to trust Him. She said "yes":

"I am the Lord's servant. Let this thing you have said happen to me!"

And so she became pregnant. As proof of unwed motherhood grew obvious to all, she surely felt the sting of censure from neighbors. To have lived a faultless life, yet to be perceived as a fallen woman, must have humiliated and exasperated her. But to her cousin Elizabeth she said, "I praise the Lord with all my heart. I am very happy because God is my Savior. I am not important, but He has shown His care for me, his lowly servant. From now until the end of time, people will remember how much God blessed me."

Mary was human. Can we even imagine her rising fear as she approached her delivery? In those days, women often died in child-birth. On a road far from home, attempting to stay astride a donkey as Joseph walked by her side, she felt the first pangs of labor. As they finally entered into a town, they were distressed to find it was overrun with travelers. As Joseph searched fruitlessly for a room, she must have felt herself in mortal danger. But she trusted God (and Joseph, who did what he could). In time, a stable was secured for the night. There, she gave birth to the Christ child that lives on in all of us.

And so began the greatest drama in history. On came the day that Mary and Joseph brought the infant Jesus to the temple. In the court-yard, the prophet Simeon shared with Mary a prophecy that must have shaken her to the core: "This child is destined to cause many in Israel to fall, and many others to rise. He has been sent as a sign from God, but many will oppose him. As a result, the deepest thoughts of many hearts will be revealed. And a sword will pierce your very soul."

For Mary, it must have felt like a sword to her soul when word came: King Herod was out to kill her baby. She and Joseph fled to Egypt with infant Jesus, where they lived until Herod died. She and Joseph taught their child His first steps and words all alone, as aliens in a for-eign land.

Oh, the fears of a parent. Years later, on a caravan journey with other travelers on the road back to Nazareth, twelve-year old Jesus slipped away– and Mary and Joseph couldn't find Him for three days. What dread she must have felt. They finally tracked Him down in Jerusalem, in the temple, teaching the scholars. Surely Mary wondered: who is this child?

Even in Jesus' adult life, Mary wrestled with fears. As she witnessed His first miracle, it must have crossed her mind that such power would bring enemies. It was at the Wedding at Cana. Remember the story? A miracle was called for, and when Jesus expressed hesitations about beginning His ministry ("my time has not yet come"), she dismissed His doubts. Despite her fear, she turned to the servants who had run out of wine and said, "Do what He tells you."

We don't often think of it this way, but this was an act of great leadership. A good leader knows when the time has come to let go, empower and get out of the way. Despite the risks. Mary knew, and Mary did.

As a servant leader, Mary supported Jesus' ministry at every step– despite her fears. She knew His divinity; she knew her own calling. But still, those fears could only have grown as the crowds began to grow– especially as the authorities reacted to His rising popularity with rising suspicion and alarm. Nothing could have prepared her for what happened upon Jesus' return to Jerusalem. To see Him welcomed by huge crowds as He entered the city. To see Him speaking truth to power. To see the rage of those in power. To see one of his closest disciples betray Him.

Mary was human. This was her Son, who she loved beyond measure. What fear she must have felt as He was dragged before the religious authorities, and later, Pontius Pilate. She saw Him scourged by whips, until His flesh began to shred. She saw Him paraded through the crowds, and taken to the cross. Mother Mary witnessed all of it. Did a sword not pierce her soul at every whiplash, at every bloodied step towards Cavalry, at every hammered nail, at every cry of pain? Yet somehow she found a courage that surpassed her fear.

Mother Mary attended her Son's crucifixion. We don't talk about it much, but its effects have echoed across time. Just a few of Jesus' followers remained by her side. As the cross was raised with Jesus on it, they must have eyed her closely. In that moment, Mary was utterly weak; utterly powerless. But God teaches that in weakness there is strength; that power comes from powerlessness. And so it is recorded in John 19:25:

"Jesus' mother stood near His cross."

Take note. Mary *stood*. She did not fall to the ground in hysterics. She did not run away. She did not rush the guards. Powerless, cut to the heart, anguished, defiant, she stood in silent witness to the terrible act. What an exhibition of leadership.

As the sun fell and her slight frame cast a vigilant shadow at the foot of the Cross, what went through the minds of Jesus' disciples? Surely Mary's courage gave courage to them. At their weakest moment, their faiths shaken to the core, their commitment to Jesus wavering, her silent defiance spoke:

"See what He has done for you.
See how much He loves you.
He believes in you; He has given His life for you.
Now serve Him; follow Him."

As Jesus took His last breath, Mary could never have imagined that three days later He would rise. She could not have known that her Son's followers, down to a handful, would mobilize a movement that would someday grow into billions. Despite all she didn't know in the seminal moments of her life, Mary knew God. When fear lurked at the edge of her heart, Mary knew where to go.

Mary's witness transformed those gathered around her. And it does the same for us. Through story and reverence, her exemplary leadership continues to transform today. Mary, the mother of Jesus, was a great leader– a leader of goodness. And the world is forever changed.

"Fear not, for I am with you; be not dismayed, for I am your God; I will strengthen you, I will help you, I will uphold you with my righteous right hand."-- Isaiah 41:10

Yours in radical surrender,

Tom

Week 52 -- Faith

THE MOMENT IS NOW

The moment is now. The onslaught's begun
Come fast to the breach, come shore up the line
Take the flag, take the lead, rally and run
It's love when you fight for justice divine

The moment is now. Need calls from the streets
Come as a servant, to work with the poor
Be bearer of hope to all whom you meet
So your good might give glimpses of God's grandeur

The moment is now, brief visitor sublime!
Run to the sorrow; it hides in plain sight
Wait not for a more convenient time
For someone's in need of your love tonight

You were born for this moment in history
See need, take wing, and fly to the mystery

Rising Leader,

Over two thousand years ago, in a desolate shed near Bethlehem, a child was born. Transcendent God humbled Himself, stepping down from Heaven to enter our world. God lived with us in human flesh for a fleeting moment, and the world was forever changed.

This Christmas, as we look upon the infant Jesus lying in some manger in some floodlit nativity scene, let us celebrate much more the birth of Christ in us. This is the birth that matters most. The star-over-Bethlehem epiphany story is meaningful if and only if it leads us to our own epiphany. Christ is in us in this right-now moment. Sense Him? He is the sap of love that pulses through us— the love that draws us back to our original goodness.

This is our faith. Our Christian faith, handed down through the ages. A faith to be grabbed onto, like a rock in the storm. It's a faith that helps us, in the words of Brother Lawrence, to "slip back into that center." Only in God is our soul at rest. Only in God may we be opened so completely that we step out of and beyond ourselves. Only in God may our circle of care become so wide it embraces the whole hurting world. Until our very lives become worship.

Great leaders can move mountains. Which is a good thing, because mountains must be moved. We are running out of time to turn the tide on climate change. Our world is closer to nuclear war than at any time in the past sixty years. We face clear and present threats to sacred American democracy. Bigotry, injustice and racial inequity are weakening too many communities. Houses of worship are shrinking inward as members flee the pews. Religious intolerance is fracturing civility. The need for charity is everywhere. For all these reasons, the time has come for all the myopic, timid, small-minded, self-absorbed, greedy, unprincipled leaders of the world to stand down. The torch must pass to a new generation of leaders.

But not just any leaders– ethical ones. Like you. To be an ethical leader takes discipline; for a Christian it takes prayer and deep soul-contemplation. Only there, in the silence of our hearts, will we begin to sense that God loves us infinitely. That He cares about every hair on our heads. Only there can we receive His light of truth– to better see our sins and sinful patterns, so we can repent. Only there can we receive His grace– that shackle-shattering God-love that sets us free. Only there can we hear, if we listen closely, the still, small whisper of His call– naming our purpose, our life meaning. Remember the challenge:

Leader of goodness,
Go in faith
To love and heal the world

That's it in a nutshell, good leader. Without God, we are lost and in the shadow of death. We become focused on ourselves– our egos. We shrink our circles of care. But with Him we are found; we are filled with new life. Faith renews us. We are born again so that we can bring rebirth to the world. Remember the disciplines of goodness? It all flows up:

It all begins with God. Lived faith (piety) is the foundation for a life of goodness. It stirs the fire of love, which moves us to stir the fire of change. Stir the fire, good leader. Let the embers of your love rise as beacons in the night sky. My generation is moving on. It's up to you.

Dag Hammarskjold described it this way: "Hold out the chalice of your being to receive, to carry, and give back."

Pray to God as Thomas Merton did: "The fact that I think I am following Your will does not mean that I am actually doing so. But I believe that the desire to please You does in fact please You. And I hope I have that desire in all that I am doing."

Remember what Mother Teresa said: "God did not call me to be successful– He called me to be faithful." The magnitude of your impact is not of your concern. Do your part, and leave the rest up to God.

You are the light this world so desperately needs. The moment is now. Step up, step out and give it your all. Jesus is calling; you are the answer.

For God so loved the world that He gave His only begotten Son, that whoever believes in Him should not perish but have everlasting life.-- John 3:16

Yours in Christ,
Tom

LETTERS TO RISING LEADERS

ACKNOWLEDGEMENTS

This book would not have been possible without the support of many people.

First off, I wish to acknowledge my good friend Steve Hayes, who spent many hours throughout late 2021 and all of 2022, reading and critiquing every letter in this book. Steve has an ad agency background, so he understands the power of the written word. His feedback was invaluable: precise, corrective, frequently bracing, and always supportive. Steve challenged me to sharpen my points, tighten my wording and, wherever possible, shorten. Many key decisions that pertained to the sequencing and themes of the letters (and the stories told within them) were influenced by him.

My wife, Pageen Mohr, provided outstanding feedback on many of my letters. She has a deep instinct for the reader's perspective, and has no tolerance for vagueness. The letters would have been far less impactful without her. My daughter Mary Catherine Mohr helped me think through the letter sequencing– both the quarterly themes and the topics of each of the letters themselves. My son Jack Mohr read through and commented on a number of the critical early letters. I am blessed to have such a talented and supportive family.

In my own faith formation, I have been influenced by many. My wife Pageen, of course– who first led me back to weekly church attendance, and whose relationship with God is rich and deep. Fr. Arnold Weber, our parish priest at Holy Name of Jesus Church in Medina, MN in the years when our kids were growing up, was a leader of goodness who taught the love of Jesus through words and action. More recently, I have learned much from Fr. Brendan McGuire, pastor of St. Simon's parish in Los Altos, CA– whose love of Jesus, generosity of heart and deep wisdom teaches so well.

Brenda and John Coleman invited Pageen and me to the Cursillo retreat that changed our lives. It was a pivotal moment in my faith journey. Through Cursillo, I came to know Hal Lance, Tim and Ro

Weldon, and many others who have left the mark of their goodness on me. Many years later, just before Covid shut everything down, Sarah and David George, Dave Roberts, Mike Haas, Darnell Johnson and Francis Matus welcomed me into and taught me about Kairos prison ministry. Due to them, I had a deeply formative experience on a weekend retreat inside Salinas Valley State Prison. Over the years, I've benefited from many deep faith discussions held with Mike and Missy Petrak, Mitch and Kris Avery and their adult children (Kit and Annika), and other good friends. Each week, I meet with a group of guys (they know who they are) who help me as I try to stay on God's path. I'm thankful for the support and accountability we share with each other.

I have been enriched by the wisdom of many Christian authors, including C.S. Lewis, Dag Hammarskjold, Rick Warren, Brian McLaren, Fr. Richard Rohr, Fr. Ron Rolheiser, and Fr. James Martin, S.J. Their influences appear throughout this book. Music has also played an important part in my faith formation. I have been especially inspired by the music of Rich Mullins, Amy Grant, Zach Williams, Lauren Daigle, Michael W. Smith, Bart Millard and Chris Tomlin.

For all of these and more, I am deeply grateful.

ABOUT ME

I live with my wife, Pageen, in Orono, MN. We are parishioners at Holy Name of Jesus Catholic Church in Medina. We have two grown children– Dr. Mary Catherine Mohr, and Jack Mohr (married to Ellie; now blessed with our first grandchild, Madeline Anne Mohr). These three millennials I love so much and know so well give me great hope for our future. They embrace the best values of their generation.

If I'm known at all in the public domain, it is because of my five business books (*Scaling the Revenue Engine*, *People Design*, *Funding & Exits*, *The Fit Systems Enterprise* and *The Four-Way Fit*). I'm a former president of a Fortune 500 subsidiary; I founded a moderately successful tech startup. For the past ten years I have served as a business coach to tech company CEOs.

But business is just one facet of my life. Christian, husband, father, sibling, friend, neighbor, musician, American citizen, global citizen– all of these roles are also part of who I am. For me, "child of God" is my most important role. I seek to know God's will in my life, and to follow it as best I can. This is what led me to write the letters, poems and songs that make up the *Rising Leader Series* and this book. I want to encourage you and other next-generation leaders to discover God, welcome Him into your hearts, and then rise up to heed God's call:

Leader of goodness,
Go in faith
To love and heal the world